BREAKTHROUGH
STRATEGIES

BREAKTHROUGH STRATEGIES

Classroom-Based Practices to Support New Majority College Students

Kathleen A. Ross

HARVARD EDUCATION PRESS
CAMBRIDGE, MASSACHUSETTS

Paperback ISBN 978-1-61250-997-6
Library Edition ISBN 978-1-61250-998-3

Library of Congress Cataloging-in-Publication Data
Names: Ross, Kathleen A., author.
Title: Breakthrough strategies : classroom-based practices to support New
    Majority college students / Kathleen A. Ross.
Description: Cambridge, Massachusetts : Harvard Education Press, [2016] |
    Includes bibliographical references and index.
Identifiers: LCCN 2016022263| ISBN 9781612509976 (pbk.) |
    ISBN 9781612509983 (library edition)
Subjects: LCSH: Minority college students—United States—Attitudes. |
    Minority college students—United States—Psychology. | Teacher-student
    relationships—United States. | Multicultural education—United States. |
    College integration—United States.
Classification: LCC LC3731 .R68 2016 | DDC 378.1/982—dc23
    LC record available at https://lccn.loc.gov/2016022263

Published by Harvard Education Press,
an imprint of the Harvard Education Publishing Group

Harvard Education Press
8 Story Street
Cambridge, MA 02138

Cover Design: Ciano Design
Cover Photo: © Simon Jarratt/Corbis

The typefaces used in this book are ITC Stone Serif, ITC Stone Sans, and ITC
Franklin Gothic BT.

CONTENTS

FOREWORD

Nearly twenty years ago, I began my career in higher education at King's College—a Catholic liberal arts college in Wilkes-Barre, Pennsylvania. I worked in the division of student affairs, in the office of multicultural and international affairs. Given my interest in diversity and equity, landing this job right out of college was a dream come true. I was excited and eager to make a difference! I worked at King's for nearly four years, and while I think I made a difference, the impact the job made on me was probably more significant.

At King's, my work focused on students, in particular racial/ethnic minorities and international students. Nearly all of these students were low-income and first-generation, and for a few, English was their second language. Prior to taking the job I had of course been a student myself, so I assumed working with students would be easy. I was surprised to find it wasn't. I quickly learned that working in service to students was definitely different than just being one. I realized that my position necessitated a heightened level of awareness and sensitivity to their needs. Even though I possessed many of the demographic characteristics of my students—namely, coming from a low-income, minority background—I still had a lot to learn.

I embraced each and every opportunity to learn about the institutional policies and practices for helping disadvantaged students get to and through college. I often found myself going beyond the borders of the division of student affairs and partnering with faculty and other institutional leaders in my attempt to make the campus more responsive to the needs of diverse students. In doing so, I realized that even though some faculty and staff desired to support these students, they had absolutely no clue of where and how to start.

During my time at King's, it was impossible to anticipate how critical those experiences would be in shaping my understanding and approach to work that would come later. But as I look back, nearly two decades later, I recognize that King's informed and deepened the commitments that drive my work today with the Institute for Higher Education Policy (IHEP). At IHEP, we focus on issues of college access and success with an emphasis on policy and its effect on underserved student populations. As a part of our work, we monitor trends in higher education, such as the ever-increasing diversity of college campuses. For example, today's students are noticeably more diverse than previous generations in terms of race, socioeconomic status, age, and family educational background.

The growing diversity of our colleges and universities is important, as these institutions should reflect the diversity of the broader society. Given that fact, our institutions must educate all students to be productive members of society, offering them opportunities to contribute to the workforce and economic development. However, we are falling short in this regard. The college attainment rate is too low, and for those from diverse backgrounds the numbers are even lower, resulting in equity gaps that have the potential to further stratify society and weaken the US economy.

In this book, *Breakthrough Strategies*, Sister Kathleen Ross offers a blueprint for helping to close these attainment gaps by increasing students' academic engagement. The book is geared toward faculty and the teaching strategies they can use to better educate today's low-income, first-generation students, whom she calls the "New Majority." Having cofounded Heritage College (now Heritage University) to provide educational opportunities to the families of the geographically isolated Yakima Valley, Sister Kathleen has firsthand knowledge in helping today's students and deeply understands the importance of education for reducing poverty and increasing opportunity. In my roles at IHEP and the US Department of Education, I have had the privilege of working with Sister Kathleen and the Heritage team. Through the years, I have watched her commitment to expanding opportunity and success for her students position her as a key voice for change in her region, among peer institutions, and nationwide.

In many ways, King's College and Heritage University are similar. They both were founded by religious orders to serve the low-income and working-class families of their respective regions. And over time, with increasing need and greater diversity, the institutions welcomed other groups of students. Many colleges and universities today are experiencing similar trends, requiring more institutional leaders to invest time and energy into learning about the New Majority and how to create learning environments that optimize their success. This book, informed by Sister Kathleen's years of experience and by her deep commitment to serving low-income students, offers instructive tools and strategies to maximize the success of today's students.

College leaders tend to bifurcate issues of student success by relegating efforts of diversity and inclusion to student affairs, thereby allowing faculty to focus on such issues only as their interest dictates. Or, faculty are given mandates to address issues of equity without being provided the tools or skills that may be intuitive to the student affairs staff steeped in this work. These strategies have never been optimal, and today, with an increasingly diverse student body, a disjointed approach to student success is not viable. Instead, faculty and student affairs professionals must work more cooperatively. Faculty, in particular, must have a centralized role in student success efforts and must be given the charge along with the tools necessary to be successful in this role. After all, faculty members are the primary point of contact for students and can provide a strong connection between learning that occurs both inside and outside the classroom.

Although more faculty need to be engaged in student success, momentum is already building for support of faculty-led efforts that increase students' academic engagement, such as the use of high-impact practices that promote curricular change and the use of new instructional approaches. Many faculty are becoming more responsive to the cultural dynamics and experiences that students bring with them to the classroom and aim to create inclusive classroom cultures, where student differences are recognized as strengths. Some faculty are also reflecting on their own cultural experiences and biases using the classroom experience to not only engage students, but also develop their own capacity to see and appreciate difference. In this book, Sister Kathleen narrates the experiences of such faculty members who have been involved in Heritage University's Breakthrough Strategies Project.

It is refreshing to see faculty from Heritage University taking proactive steps to foster student success. The benefits of improving the educational attainment of the New Majority are important not only for individual students and society, but also for the institutions where they enroll. Institutions that devote time and target resources to better support these students have a much better chance of achieving optimal results around institutional and student success goals.

This book offers examples and strategies that can increase student engagement and success. These strategies, developed and tested at Heritage University, can be easily replicated and scaled at other institutions seeking to increase the academic success of the New Majority and other students. This work is not easy, but the return on investment will be great, in terms of both increasing students' academic progress and fostering a campus culture that understands students and supports collaboration and learning.

Michelle Asha Cooper, PhD
President, Institute for Higher Education Policy
Washington, DC

CHAPTER 1

The Breakthrough Strategies Project

Most educated adults have accepted the often-cited fact that America will be a "majority-minority" country by 2050.[1] But many otherwise well-informed college faculty and administrators haven't fully grasped the significance of this reality as it affects their work with college-going individuals. It is precisely this cohort of students that is leading the population shift to "majority-minority" status, and importantly, changing the face of college classrooms. Nor have we educators fully recognized that a much larger proportion of those who come from Latino/a, African American, Native American, and Southeast Asian/Pacific Islander families are low-income and first-generation-to-college than among white and Asian populations.[2] In other words, this demographic shift results in a change not only in ethnicity but also in socioeconomic and family education status among the younger generations.

In fact, for many institutions of higher education, the "New Majority" students currently enrolling or very shortly expected to arrive in greater numbers are first-generation-to-college, low-income students. One simple statistic illustrates this fact. In 2002–03 the number of eligible applicants to the federal Pell Grant financial aid program was

4.8 million, which was 23 percent of the 20.7 million undergraduates enrolled over that twelve-month period. The Pell Grant is a good surrogate measure of low-income status. Ten years later, in 2012–13, the total undergraduate enrollment had grown to 24.8 million and the number of eligible Pell Grant applicants had jumped to 8.9 million or 36 percent of the twelve-month enrollment. In other words, the percentage of Pell Grant applicants increased more than 50 percent in that ten-year period.[3] Yet during that same period, the number of Americans between the ages of fifteen and twenty-four only grew by 2.6 percent, and the total higher education enrollment grew only by 19.8 percent. The difference illustrates the phenomenon of the New Majority coming to college.

While this change in demographics is now seeping into the consciousness of college faculty and administrators, many are focusing on the weaknesses in the K–12 educational experiences of these students, especially those coming from low-income neighborhoods and under-resourced schools. Most of their efforts are concentrated on students not prepared to enter college-level courses. They are especially concerned with the high numbers who don't have the minimum competencies necessary to succeed in basic English composition classes, entry-level courses in mathematics, and survey courses in the humanities, sciences, and social sciences. To deal with this, some institutions are inaugurating or expanding "bridge" classes held prior to the beginning of the school year or even during students' senior year in high school. Heritage University, an institution I cofounded, where the vast majority of undergraduates fit the profile of the New Majority student, has been experimenting with this approach for several years, creating various versions of bridge programs in math and writing, and tracking the success of these programs in getting students ready for college-level courses as soon as they enroll as full-time college students.[4] Another approach utilized by many institutions is placing students in remedial or developmental courses that do not carry credit toward a college degree.[5]

Some may think that if one or the other of these approaches is active on their campus, so that first-gen students enter their college-level classes only after having scored high enough on an entrance test, or passed a bridge program course or a remedial course provided by the college, then the problem of assuring that first-gen students have an equal chance to succeed with non-first-gen students is solved. To be sure, it is encouraging to see in recent higher education conferences and literature a great deal of creative thinking and experimenting being applied to the challenge of providing remedial courses or bridge programs to assure the success of New Majority students in college, but these approaches are not sufficient. There is another level of challenge facing first-gen students that often goes unrecognized.

This book was written to raise awareness among college faculty and provide them with research-based strategies for helping New Majority students overcome a different set of barriers that are as inimical to success in college as the lack of academic readiness, if not more so. I am speaking about significant cultural barriers that exist due to the differences between the dominant current college setting—a middle-class professional environment—and the working-class background of New Majority students. To a large extent, faculty and administrators are unaware of or poorly prepared to deal with these differences between the sociocultural milieu of the New Majority students and the college world. True, there is widespread concern about the financial stresses of many New Majority students, and there are numerous commendable efforts to solve students' immediate financial needs. This is indeed important. But when I say "sociocultural world," I am referring to the rest of a whole universe of interpersonal and social conventions, norms, and expectations that the New Majority students bring with them to college and that differ in significant ways from those embodied in the typical college setting. Most middle-class people, college faculty and administrators included, are not aware that there are significant differences beyond just financial resources that distinguish the working-class sociocultural world from the typical middle-class world in which most faculty and administrators grew up and currently live. And these differences can be enormous in the college experience of, and therefore the success rate of, New Majority students. As Professor Nicole Stephens of Northwestern University has noted in reporting on multiple research projects she and her colleagues conducted:

One critical factor underlying the social class achievement gap is American universities' focus on middle-class norms of independence as the culturally appropriate way to be a college student. Research suggests that this focus is likely to seem natural or normative to continuing-generation students from middle-class backgrounds . . . but present a relative mismatch for students from working-class backgrounds. Further, [our] research examines how seemingly neutral cultural norms, once institutionalized, can systematically produce differences in achievement.[6]

A key place on campus where these differences inevitably come into play is in the typical college classroom. For instance, I have heard many New Majority students talking about their fear of asking questions in front of others. "My parents always taught me, 'Don't ask questions in front of people smarter than you are; you'll just look stupid.'" How does this play out in a typical university classroom with a significant number of New Majority students? The professor might plan a class session to begin with a carefully developed presentation for thirty minutes, to be followed by twenty minutes of answering students' questions. But when he finishes the presentation and then can't coax any questions from his students even when he tells them "There are no dumb questions," he is confused and discouraged. It is puzzling and unnerving to this college professor whose parents encouraged and rewarded smart questions from their children and who is unaware of the opposite norm that his first-gen students have heard many times from their parents.

We've seen another unexpected difference in New Majority students who exclaim how shocked they are that a big paper is due next week. My first question back to them is always, "Didn't you get a syllabus at the beginning of this course?" And a typical answer is, "I didn't know what a syllabus is for. I guess I was supposed to read it on my own and notice these deadlines for the big assignments! I thought the professor would tell us a lot more in class about any big assignment and keep reminding us of the date." Having never heard her parents talk about college courses or course syllabi, a first-gen student hasn't experienced the context that would prepare her to check the syllabus and note in her calendar the major assignments. These examples and many others illustrate that students have absorbed messages from their non-college-experienced families that differ markedly from those learned by most professors as young people in their college-educated families and their years in the professoriate.

Because most faculty are not aware of the numerous, mostly subliminal differences characterizing middle-class versus working-class behavior norms, mindsets, and expectations, they are also unaware of how these often subtle factors in the students' sociocultural world can work against their classroom success. These differences can cause frustrations and misjudgments on the part of students' professors as well. This can be true, no matter how discipline-competent, well-meaning, and devoted faculty members are.

This is the reality that I, who came from a middle-class college-going family, have discovered over thirty-five years of serving at Heritage University in rural Washington State. From its beginning the mission has been to focus on providing quality higher education opportunities to those who have been educationally isolated for geographic, economic, and cultural reasons. For the past thirty-five years, more than 80 percent of Heritage's undergraduates have been low-income, and about 85 percent are the first in their families to pursue a four-year degree. In addition, 60–70 percent of the students come from ethnicities whose average college degree attainment is significantly lower than the national average, reflecting families without college-going experience.[7] As Heritage University consistently enrolls a New Majority undergraduate student body, its professors strongly embrace the University's mission, which focuses on these students. The faculty are constantly experimenting, reflecting, and sharing successful classroom strategies through the work of the university's dynamic Center for Intercultural Learning and Teaching.

Heritage University's track record with nurturing successful alumni is something that frequently brings us great satisfaction and encouragement. Former students doing well in their careers contact us, telling about their children who are now planning college applications or are already attending. They tell us about serving on town or county committees and organizations as well as their commitment to improving their local communities. And they tell us about their unfailing gratitude.

We also see encouraging improvements in services and opportunities throughout our region, thanks to Heritage graduates. For instance, when Heritage launched its social work program in the early 1990s, no social service agency in our entire ninety-mile Yakima Valley had any professional staff who were able to serve Spanish-speaking clients in their native language. Thanks to adding a nationally accredited program in social work almost twenty years ago, and the dedication and teaching skill of Heritage University faculty, within about a dozen years every social service agency in the Valley had at least one Spanish-speaking professional. Virtually all of these new professionals came from first-gen families and were not only able to counsel families in their maternal language but could also tap into their own first-generation and low-income backgrounds to provide relevant and effective services. We have seen similar results as first-gen graduates have become K–12 teachers as well as school principals, new business owners, attorneys, community leaders, and professionals in many other fields, including with Fortune 500 companies.

In the media and political venues, graduation rates are often used as a measure of an institution's success. While the metrics of calculating graduation rates are under discussion and need improvement, these data points are still a touchstone for discussing success. Heritage University continues to work diligently on improving our graduation rates, even though our rates are frequently at least double those achieved by low-income, first-gen students nationally. Yet we are not at all satisfied or complacent, because our rates, as well as the statistics underlying the reality for New Majority students nationwide, are shockingly low. According to the *Pell Institute's 2011 Fact Sheet*, the graduation rates for low-income, first-generation students earning a baccalaureate degree within six years of enrolling in postsecondary education was only 10.9 percent.[8] In 2015, the report produced by the Pell Institute with the University of Pennsylvania Alliance stated that as of 2013 only 9 percent of twenty-four-year-olds from families in the lowest family income quartile had earned a four-year degree.[9] Virtually all of Heritage's students fall into the category of low-income, first-generation. In 2014, 91 percent of our entering students received Pell Grants, indicating their low-income status, and approximately 85 percent indicated they were first-gen students. Yet Heritage's six-year graduation rate is double the national rate of four-year degree attainment. As of 2013, Heritage's six-year rate was 19 percent. Moreover, the eight-year graduation rate at Heritage is 30 percent, and the ten-year rate is 35 percent. This does not include the significant numbers who transfer to another institution and complete a degree that Heritage does not offer.[10] (No comparable national eight-year or ten-year data are available.) An obvious explanation for the 85 percent increase in the graduation rate (from 19 percent to 35 percent) by the tenth year after initial enrollment is the reality that almost all Heritage University students work while attending school, with more than half of them employed at full-time jobs. This is also the case for many low-income, first-gen students attending higher education institutions nationally.[11]

THE ORIGINS OF THIS BOOK

In 2010 I completed twenty-eight years as the president of Heritage University and was delighted to help inaugurate its second president, who had broad experience in higher education, to take Heritage to its next level of development.[12] I saw myself beginning an exploration of ways in which I could perhaps translate the unique experiences of Heritage University in educating students we now recognize as New Majority into useful information and insights to share with faculty in other institutions who are beginning to enroll substantial numbers of these students. My early research focused on reviewing the literature about today's college students, especially those with a New Majority background. I was looking in particular at their success or failure to achieve the degrees they set out to obtain, and at current efforts to find solutions to the troubling graduation rates reported in the literature.

While I was on sabbatical as a visiting research professor at Claremont Graduate University in 2011, I learned that there were extensive efforts to address the needs of New Majority students underway on many levels of the admissions, advising, and student services programs at a large number of colleges and universities. But my research indicated that few of those efforts addressed, or even explored, what happens to students inside their college classrooms and in their relationships with their professors. As I was becoming more and more convinced that this gap existed in the current research and campus-based projects, a publication of the Institute for Higher Education Policy, *Supporting First-Generation College Students Through Classroom-Based Practices*, confirmed my findings and reported the same conclusion.[13] This galvanized my energy when I returned to Heritage University to start the Institute for Student Identity and Success. A significant grant from the College Spark Washington Foundation allowed me to begin employing a few grant-funded research assistants who were all New Majority students.

At the Institute, we focused on practical research aimed at identifying effective faculty strategies that were being employed inside Heritage classrooms and labs to facilitate the success of first-generation students. As we planned our methods of inquiry, we reviewed a number of publications to be sure we were attuned to all the factors that we should look for once we started gathering information on campus. I synthesized our findings from a review of the literature into four categories of experiences that are essential for New Majority students to achieve college success. These four are engaged learning, feeling connected with faculty and fellow students, academic self-confidence, and a vision of what college success could enable the student to do and to be. We summarized these as Engagement, Belonging, Confidence, and Vision. After being invited to give presentations about this initial research at several regional higher education events and conferences, and hearing the questions and frequent surprise coming from higher education leaders as they learned about some of the barriers faculty face in implementing these "Four Essentials," I became highly motivated to find and describe as many helpful, practical faculty practices to address these as I could, so they could be shared with faculty at other institutions.

The idea of writing a series of briefing papers began to surface at that point. In reviewing the research available in 2012 and 2013, the lack of information was obvious regarding classroom strategies that would be effective with New Majority students in these crucial Four Essentials. It was also obvious that there were (and continue to be) many faculty who were well prepared and active in their disciplines, as well as being very committed to student success, who had no opportunity to learn about strategies specifically geared to creating success for students from non-college-going and low-income families. When I tested out the idea of creating tip sheets with faculty at Heritage and elsewhere, the reaction was supportive but reserved. When I probed a bit, someone said, "Tip sheets will get put into a pile of unread material on professors' desks. Why don't you make three-minute videos that they can just click on?" The immediate result of these conversations, coupled with the availability of grant funding, served to focus us on producing with a professional videographer very short (three to four minutes) videos to demonstrate some of the strategies.[14] Those videos received national visibility and sparked feedback from various people around the country, indicating that a book might be very useful by providing more substantial explanations about helpful strategies for student success in the Four Essentials.

Identifying Breakthrough Strategies

But I am getting ahead of the story. Just how did I identify the strategies that are the basis for this book? Inspired by a dream of helping faculty achieve greater success with New Majority students, I began a search for specific strategies used by faculty *that students themselves identified as significant to their success.* Fortunately, I had effective assistance from student research assistants (RAs) at our Institute who collected information directly from their peers. I trained them to do anonymous, informal oral interviews, in a "man-on-the-street" format. They hung out in the dining hall or in hallways as classes dismissed or engaged students briefly as they walked across campus. Originally the RAs wrote answers to their simple questions on notepaper, but soon they moved to recording the interviews, still anonymous, on their cell phones and then transcribing them. Two basic questions they used were, "Have you had a professor who went 'above and beyond' to help you succeed in a class? What did he or she do?" Another two were, "In what class have you learned the most since you came to Heritage University? What was it about this class that helped you learn so much?" The RA followed up the interviewees' brief answers with exploratory probes designed to elicit specifics about what strategies and approaches the professor employed. Two other institutions joined us in our research—Yakima Valley Community College in Yakima, Washington, and Holy Names University in Oakland, California—and students there were also trained to conduct student focus groups using similar questions that addressed the research goal of finding effective teaching practices.

More than a hundred interviews at Heritage University, and focus groups of students at Yakima Valley Community College and Holy Names University, over a period of two years yielded a list of faculty whom students mentioned repeatedly, along with intriguing references to particular strategies the faculty used to support students. We reviewed the interview results to focus on those faculty receiving the most mention and strongest affirmations. We noted enthusiastic endorsements from students, but their descriptions of exactly what they found helpful were often hard to visualize. This led to the next step. I conducted in-depth interviews with the most frequently mentioned faculty who appeared to be using strategies we judged could be applicable across more than one discipline so they could be used by as many college faculty as possible.

Accompanied by one or more RAs, I engaged each of these faculty members in a probing conversation, usually about ninety minutes, to investigate further the strategies that had been mentioned by students. We were often surprised by the end of these interviews to learn that the faculty member had not specifically designed, nor in some cases even recognized, the exact nature of the strategy that he or she was using. It had just evolved from teaching experiences with these New Majority students and had become part of the repertoire that the professor integrated within other teaching approaches. It took an outsider like me asking questions to motivate professors to articulate exactly why and how their strategies are effective.

Through this two-step "action research" we narrowed our focus to insightful strategies that could be used across a variety of disciplines, which we called Breakthrough Strategies. We also sought to identify faculty willing to speak about their strategies in short videos (three to four minutes), which could easily be shared with new faculty coming to Heritage and indeed with faculty anywhere, via the Heritage University website and YouTube. Thus the *Breakthrough Strategies Videos* were birthed.

After the first eight videos were posted in July 2013, we began to receive feedback from viewers throughout the country, and it was overwhelmingly positive. We also heard that the viewers were intrigued by the underlying motivations for each of the strategies described. They had questions about various details of implementing the strategies that could not be addressed in a three- or four-minute video. At that point we began to consider the possibility of preparing a book describing the strategies, the rationales behind them, and why they are especially important for New Majority students.

Viewers also wanted to know why or whether these practical actions by professors were showing good results. To address this question, we did a statistical analysis whereby we compared the pass rate in courses taught by the professors who used the strategies we highlighted in the videos with the pass rate in the same courses taught by other Heritage University faculty. The analysis addressed a total of 553 student enrollments in the two sets of courses. The courses ranged across a number of disciplines from science to business to humanities. A correlation analysis by our Institutional Research Office revealed that 9 percent of those taking the class from a professor who used one or more of the Breakthrough Strategies failed the class, while 18 percent who took the same course from a professor not familiar with the Breakthrough Strategies failed to earn a passing grade. This difference, when statistically analyzed, had a p value of .017, showing that it is statistically significant at the <.05 level, and it encouraged us to continue pursuing these teaching strategies and related classroom approaches.[15] Now we knew we needed to do more analysis of the strategies that the highlighted professors were using, and we became convinced that this information would be helpful to faculty in any college or university that faces a significant uptick in the percentage of students coming from New Majority backgrounds.

As we analyzed our interview transcripts and faculty conversation notes, we realized that probing in more detail the realities in the lives of New Majority students would be necessary to help our colleagues understand what makes these Breakthrough Strategies so relevant and important. With this mandate in mind, and with encouragement from the Harvard Education Press, we began developing the full content of this book.

HOW TO USE THIS BOOK

The readers I hope to reach through this book are current college and university faculty who find they are teaching more and more students who are New Majority. Doctoral students who are preparing to become professors, especially those who do not receive a great deal of training in pedagogy and educational theory, should also benefit from this book. They will gain some practical insights regarding their future students—how to understand them and how to reach them.

Many colleges and universities now have something akin to Heritage University's Center for Intercultural Teaching and Learning (CILT), which is dedicated to faculty development and support.[16] Staff in these resource centers may also find ideas in this book that can help solve faculty members' classroom quandaries in getting New Majority students to persevere and succeed. In orientation sessions for new faculty, these ideas may be especially helpful.

From a practical as well as theoretical point of view, most dedicated faculty do not have a lot of time to devote to the study of the pedagogical literature. They are heavily involved in keeping up with their subject matter, preparing and delivering their classes, and meeting with students. The goal of this book is to present concrete practical strategies that can readily be used, with minimal extra preparation, in many different college courses and disciplines.

How This Book Is Organized

Prior to introducing the strategies that form the core of this book, chapter 2 introduces the history of Heritage University and its unique mission. Chapter 3 explains a key concept called "communication mismatch," which undergirds many of the strategies.

The remaining chapters 4 through 14 are each devoted to one of eleven strategies that have proven to be so helpful in the college classroom. They are organized under four sections corresponding to the four essentials identified by our literature review as being critical for New Majority students in achieving college success: Engagement, Belonging, Confidence, and Vision. Each of the strategy chapters begins with a story illustrating real-life dilemmas that first-generation students often experience as a result of their lack of familiarity with college-level teaching and college classroom culture. Some of these stories are a melding of several related incidents, and some are reported pretty much as I experienced them. In the case of the opening stories, I have changed the names of the professors and students. However, with pleasure, I have included the real names of the professors whose work was identified in our research as effective, and in many cases I have included links to short videos in which they explain their strategies.

Following each opening story, I introduce an analysis of underlying factors that are creating barriers, followed by a relevant strategy or strategies that a faculty member might use to address these real-life dilemmas, including other research in addition to ours that supports the strategies as well as other alternatives for implementing the strategy where applicable. I include reflections by Heritage faculty who developed the strategies and provide opportunities for the reader to pursue them in more depth.

It is my hope that more professors will be inspired to try some of these strategies, as suitable to their various classroom and lab settings. I also hope that many will use this book as an opportunity to analyze their own most effective teaching approaches and to find ways to share them with others.

CHAPTER 2

Welcome to Heritage University

I f you've never heard of Heritage University, don't feel like you've been out of the loop or culpably unaware. Unlike the almost four-hundred-year-old other "HU" university, which everyone knows—where I spent a four-month sabbatical in 1981 while working to envision Heritage University and where this book has been published—Heritage University was founded very recently, in 1982. The circumstances that birthed it, its location in a remote part of the far western United States, and its target populations make it quite unique. However, the recent evolution of America's college-going population to include the New Majority students from low-income families where no one has previously earned a four-year degree has turned Heritage University's uniqueness into an important resource for others in higher education who want to learn how faculty can facilitate success for this group.

What could have possibly motivated sensible people to start a new four-year college in the early 1980s when the country was deep in recession, and private nonprofit colleges were closing due to financial pressures?[1] Here's the story.

Heritage University's roots go back to an institution started in 1907 by a Catholic teaching order, the Sisters of the Holy Names of Jesus and Mary, founded in Canada's rural Quebec Province in 1844 to teach the underserved; they are usually known as the Holy Names Sisters and use the initials "SNJM," from the French name of the order. In 1859 they sent a contingent of twelve young women to the Oregon Territory and established schools throughout what became the states of Washington and Oregon. In 1907 the Holy Names Sisters founded Holy Names College, with centers in Spokane and Seattle, to educate future teachers. That institution evolved into Fort Wright College of the Holy Names in 1960 when the college was awarded a seventy-five-acre portion of the recently surplused Fort Wright Air Force Base outside of Spokane. Holy Names College moved from central Spokane and renamed itself Fort Wright College of the Holy Names. Between 1960 and 1980 the college experienced early growth and then decline as more options for four-year degrees appeared in the Spokane area with the expansion of the region's state-funded higher education institutions.[2]

Part of the college's growth in the 1970s was due to an unlikely expansion into two remote areas of central Washington State, both precipitated by requests from local Native American educators. One of these was two hundred miles southwest of Spokane, where Fort Wright began offering both undergraduate and graduate education programs in 1975. This extension began in response to an urgent request from two Yakama Nation women, Martha B. Yallup and Violet Lumley Rau, founders of the first Head Start programs for the Yakama Nation, which had more than five thousand members at the time.

Martha and Violet had both earned four-year degrees by either moving away from the reservation temporarily to Ellensburg, Washington, site of the closest four-year-degree-granting institution, or making the four-hour round-trip commute there on class days. They knew that their new Head Start preschool teachers, with their own children and families to manage, could never earn degrees in the same way. Responding to their plea to develop well-educated teachers serving on the Yakama Reservation, Fort Wright College agreed to fly faculty into the nearby Yakima airport on Fridays to offer college classes in the preschool classrooms after the kids went home. These courses would ultimately, everyone hoped, lead to a baccalaureate degree in education for the participants. In addition to the tribal preschool teachers, other locals joined the classes, which grew to about thirty adults. Some of these were from the growing Mexican immigrant farm worker families.

A crisis emerged in 1980, when the administrators of the Holy Names Sisters announced that they were running out of money after picking up the college's deficit for several years, and could no longer subsidize the annual losses. They decided Fort Wright College of the Holy Names would phase out over the next eighteen months, and students were told that during this window they should complete their degrees or transfer to one of the other institutions in the Spokane area. As the academic vice president, I brought this devastating message to Martha and Violet in Toppenish, and the reaction was immediate: "You can't close this program! Our students can't finish in eighteen months; they are attending only part-time because they run our preschool full-time! And where would our students transfer to? There's no institution within commuting distance!"

Soon Martha and Violet proposed an alternative: "Let's start our own college!" My response to them was immediate: "Are you crazy?" They countered with an exclamation now emblazoned on the wall of Heritage University's Academic Skills Center: "Tell us one thing we can't do!" My answer came quickly: "We can't start a new college unless we have a board of directors willing to take on full responsibility for an expensive enterprise. Who could you find on the Yakama Reservation or in the rural Yakima Valley? You'd need experienced community leaders, people with money and willing to take on a huge responsibility."

In a matter of weeks, they shocked me by producing a list of ten signatories, including two of Yakima County's three county commissioners, the Yakima City mayor, the superintendent of the Toppenish School District, the administrator of Toppenish Community Hospital, the owners of the largest lumber business in the region, and other community leaders. Obviously, Martha and Violet were not the only ones who believed that the Yakima Valley region needed a four-year college. Before long the newly established board had met, filed nonprofit incorporation papers, and defined the mission of the new four-year college: to provide high-quality, accessible four-year and master's degrees to the multiethnic underserved population of the Yakima Valley. This included not only the Yakama Nation Reservation, but also a large and booming agricultural region where successful farms and ranches were operated by third- and fourth-generation Dutch, German, and French-Canadian immigrant families as well as the children of emigrants from the 1930s and 1940s Dust Bowl regions. The growing need for agricultural workers was fueling an influx of Mexican farm workers who lived both on and off the reservation.[3] With this ambitious vision in mind, the new board of directors chose the name "Heritage College" to reflect the expected student enrollees from various backgrounds, and they drafted me to serve as the first president.

A temporary president took over in Spokane to oversee the gradual closure of Fort Wright College (FWC) between the fall term of 1980 and the end of the 1982 spring term. In January 1981 I began a four-month sabbatical as an associate faculty member at the Harvard School of Education. Thanks to the amazing work being done back home by Martha and Violet, this quickly turned into a long-distance planning exercise to develop a strategy to turn the FWC outreach site at Toppenish into a full four-year college program. In August 1981 I moved to the Yakima Valley and began serving as the president of the Heritage Campus of Fort Wright College in Toppenish while simultaneously continuing as the academic vice president at Fort Wright College in Spokane, thus creating a transition year for the new college and enrolling about seventy-five students. Ultimately, a mostly smooth transition evolved as FWC officially closed on June 30, 1982, and the new Heritage College officially opened as an independent institution, a year after its incorporation, on July 1, 1982.

With its degree offerings expanded beyond teacher education, Heritage College enrolled approximately 120 students in 1982. The student body was about one-third Native American, one-third white, and one-third Latino/a. Within the first ten years, the student body grew to over five hundred undergraduates, with the proportion of ethnicities gradually shifting to include a larger percentage of Latinos/as and a smaller proportion of Native Americans. By 2000, the graduate programs in various teacher education specializations burgeoned and the undergraduate student body increased, bringing the student body count to more than a thousand. In 2004, Heritage College changed its name to Heritage University to reflect more accurately its offering of both undergraduate and graduate degrees. It also helped to clarify its postsecondary four-year degree status with the local Spanish-speaking population for whom the term "college" (similar to Spanish *colegio*) meant a high school rather than a postsecondary institution. In 2015, Heritage University enrolled approximately 1,200 students including almost 900 undergraduates.

The unusual story of Heritage's founding is matched by other unique characteristics. It is located on a large Indian reservation (the Yakama Nation in 2015 had almost eleven thousand enrolled members and land covering more than a million acres), but Heritage is not a tribal college owned or managed by a tribal council. Although it is a liberal arts institution that participates actively in the American Association of Colleges and Universities (AAC&U, the national liberal arts organization), it has no residence halls and all its students are commuters. As noted in chapter 1, at least 90 percent of Heritage's new undergraduates each year qualify for federal Pell Grants, a surrogate measure for being low-income, and approximately 85 percent of the undergraduates identify themselves as the first in their family who will earn a four-year degree (or as we know them, first-generation students).[4] In most years, the number of transfer students exceeds those who are enrolling in college for the first time; they come from community colleges in the region or have previously attended four-year institutions located beyond commuting distance of the Yakima Valley. The average age for the undergraduates is approximately twenty-seven, and many students "stop out" for at least one term either before transferring to Heritage or while pursuing a Heritage degree. Almost all students have some kind of outside paid employment and about half of them work full-time in addition to taking a full-time course load. To summarize, Heritage University's typical student is a commuter from a low-income family, having stopped out for at least one term along the way, holding down an outside job, and aspiring to be the first in the family to earn a four-year degree. About 70 percent are women, and half the students have children, while a good number of the remainder assist at home with younger brothers and sisters.

With this unusual student body sitting in their classrooms, Heritage University's dedicated professors have adapted their approaches while maintaining the pursuit of high standards. They have learned through trial and error as well as wonderful creativity what works to produce highly engaged, confident, connected students who become successful in earning four-year degrees and who find employment in professional roles their parents never expected to see in their families.

CHAPTER 3

Communication, Culture, and the New Majority

E ffective interactions with their professors are vital for all students to feel supported, motivated, and confident enough to meet high standards, to persevere, and to ask for help when needed. This is a special challenge for New Majority students who, compared to continuing-generation students, are less likely to have family members with the experience or knowledge to give them helpful support when communication with a professor is not going well.

We have learned from our experience and research at Heritage University that faculty who are most effective with New Majority students have come to understand that differing cultural norms were often to blame for problems in completing assignments or participating in class. These types of misunderstandings are explained eloquently by a little-discussed theory called "communication mismatch." Before introducing the strategies themselves, it is important to introduce this insightful theory and how it plays a role in interactions between faculty and students both inside and outside the classroom.

COMMUNICATION MISMATCH THEORY

Applying communication mismatch theory to the college classroom is an approach that I find most enlightening as I try to understand why we lose so many New Majority students before they complete their college programs and why others who may persevere still do not perform at their full potential. I think of this concept in a practical way that has provided me with beneficial insights I would not have otherwise gained about how the low-income, non-college-going family background of most New Majority students affects their college success efforts.

This nomenclature of "communication mismatch" may be unfamiliar to many college professors, because it is a phenomenon that was identified and labeled within the field of linguistics and is not commonly mentioned in academic literature about college teaching. I became acquainted with it through the work of John Regan, professor emeritus of linguistics, communication, and educational studies at Claremont Graduate University in California, who developed and used the concept extensively in his work across cultures in Australia and Asia.[1] I was privileged to work with him for several years and then utilized the communication mismatch theory in depth in my work with the Yakama Indian Nation from 1976 through 1979, which resulted in my dissertation, *Cultural Factors in the Success and Failure of American Indian Students in Higher Education.*[2]

The communication mismatch concept is based on a deeper analysis of the communication phenomena between any two individuals. Person A communicates something, in words and/or in body language, believing that her words and/or body language will convey to Person B the ideas and feelings and attitudes that Person A is attempting to communicate. In other words, Person A is presuming, without consciously thinking about it, that her words and body language have exactly the same meaning to Person B as they do to her. When this actually happens, this communication episode is a "communication match."

So you've probably inferred that the opposite of this is a communication mismatch. But what is it exactly, and why does it happen instead of a communication *match*?

Most of us are unaware of how a person's sum total of behavior traits and norms, which he calls upon subconsciously as he communicates, are significantly impacted by the socioeconomic, educational, and cultural setting in which he was raised and currently lives. This is succinctly noted by Richard Brislin and his colleagues in their excellent, early summary of issues surrounding the challenges of intercultural communication, *Intercultural Interactions: A Practical Guide*. Note that the term "culture" in the following excerpt is being used in the broad sense, encompassing not only language and ethnicity but also differences in socioeconomic classes and educational backgrounds.

> People typically have difficulty when moving across cultures. Suddenly, and with little warning, behaviors and attitudes that proved necessary for obtaining goals in their own culture are no longer useful. Further, familiar behaviors that marked a well-adjusted person in their own culture are seen as indicative of an ill-mannered person.[3]

Brislin is referring to ideas that generally remain just below the overt consciousness level as normal interactions go on throughout the day. Some examples of these subliminal realities are how a person uses language (formalities, slang, expletives, etc.); the meaning intended by various behaviors and body language, based on the specific setting in which the behavior occurs; the learned norms for appropriate actions in given situations; the attitudes presumed to be the same for everyone in a given setting; the past experiences of reward or punishment for specific actions or words; and behavior preferences influenced by the individual's unique personality. In ordinary communication settings, all of these subliminal factors and many more come into play without any verbalized or conscious reference to them. As Clotaire Rapaille puts it, "It is obvious to everyone that cultures are different from one another. What most people don't realize, however, is that these differences actually lead to our processing the same information in different ways."[4]

To understand the concept of communication mismatch, we'll look more closely at the unrecognized consequences of behavior traits and internal norms remaining subliminal and below the conscious level during communication events. Why is this important? Here's a practical example. If you grow up in a very low-crime, reasonably affluent neighborhood among people with high levels of education, your behavior norms and your expectations of others' behaviors will be significantly different in many areas when compared to those of a person who grows up in a low-income, frequent-turnover, low-education-level, high-crime neighborhood. An obvious example is that persons from these two different socioeconomic cultures are likely to have vastly different behavior norms and expectations about such simple things as when to lock the doors or windows of their houses, or when to close the window blinds, or whether to open their doors if a stranger knocks. Someone who has only lived in one of these settings will presume that the "normal" behavior experienced in these matters is normal everywhere. If we are aware of that single-experience background of individuals, we can anticipate that they will expect only the behavior appropriate in their own background when confronted with these ordinary household activities.

But other aspects of human interactions and expectations, which are much more subtle, are not necessarily known or presumed to be different by individuals from disparate backgrounds and realities. They are unaware of more elusive dissimilarities between themselves and others in how they view human interaction nuances and expectations. Examples are what slang or swear words are "okay" to use in what settings; when to speak up and offer your opinion and when to remain silent; whether it is acceptable to disagree with a speaker depending upon your status in relation to that speaker; what career or living setting you picture yourself in ten years from now and why; and thousands of other subliminal expectations and norms.[5] The fact that there are significant differences in these personal realities is often not evident to either party. The result is that when Person A has well-meaning intentions but her behavior transmits a meaning to Person B that differs from what she meant to convey, a misunderstanding is likely to develop. Since it is highly likely that one or both parties are unaware that the meaning of the behavior in question is understood in a different way by the other, the situation does not automatically resolve itself. Hypothetically, if Person A could fully articulate the meaning that she intended and Person

B could fully articulate the meaning that she understood from that behavior, then Person A would probably say, "Oh! That's not what I meant!" And a short clarification on both sides could end the misunderstanding. But this kind of clearly articulated knowledge sharing rarely happens because neither party is aware that it is needed. Both parties are likely to be totally unaware of the contradictory meanings imputed by the other to the behavior or language in question, and therefore both parties misunderstand the meaning of what has just happened.

This, then, is what is meant by a "communication mismatch." The intended meaning coming from Person A did not match the meaning understood by Person B. Person A did not intend to confuse or offend Person B. It happened purely as a function of the two persons having entirely different internal "dictionaries" for explaining the meaning of the external words and the body language accompanying the communication. A frequently used example of communication mismatch happening during an interpersonal communication exchange is eye contact. For instance, the difference in how someone from the middle-class white culture in the United States is socialized to use eye contact is in contrast with the norms learned in the African American family, according to research. We can start with "the dominant-culture pattern"—that of the white middle class—in which "the speaker tends to look away when speaking . . . and the listener looks directly at the speaker."[6] In a collegiate setting where both the student and the professor are from white middle-class backgrounds, a professor who is lecturing a student after class for some deficiency and notices that the student is looking directly at him would be correct in assuming that the student is accepting the criticism, since eye contact from the listener is expected.

Because of cultural differences, however, given the same scenario between a professor and student who are both African American, the professor would likely be correct in assuming that the student is resisting the criticism by maintaining eye contact. Two University of Connecticut researchers reported, "The norm governing eye contact in Black culture, then, seems to be that respect and submission are indicated by aversion of the eyes; disrespect and rebellion by a direct gaze. This norm seems to be in direct contrast with the rule governing eye contact in the White culture."[7]

Based on this assessment by Gilliam and Van Den Berg, as long as the two individuals who are interacting—in this case a professor and his student—are from the same background, the same message will be traveling back and forth between them through their words and behavior. But if the professor and student are from different backgrounds—if the professor is white and the student is African American—a communication mismatch would likely occur. The professor would read the steady eye contact from the African American student as indicating an *acceptance* of the criticism he is giving, while the student would be thinking he is communicating just the opposite, a rejection of the criticism. If you reverse the cultural backgrounds, so that the professor is an African American trying to communicate criticism to a white student who is looking at the floor, a communication mismatch would also be occurring. The white student is not accepting the criticism and therefore looking away, while the African American professor automatically assumes that this behavior indicates the student is acquiescing to this admonition. Think of this in the context of college: if the professor knows that the student is rejecting a piece of advice, he or she might take the time to explain more fully, in a way that the student might come around and see the need to, say, make class attendance a higher priority. But when the professor doesn't recognize the mismatch, he or she would likely assume that the student is now planning to change. When this does not happen on subsequent class days, the professor will feel frustrated and probably decide that it does no good to admonish this student. The potential communication connection between the professor and this student, which might have been the beginning of a crucial supportive relationship for the student, simply doesn't happen.

In my experience, this kind of mutual misunderstanding, unintentional and not verbally named or analyzed, is a much more common occurrence for New Majority students and their college professors, staff, or administrators than has been recognized. The way young people begin to solve the day-to-day challenges in their lives as they come to college is automatically influenced by their earlier life experiences, which are based on their cultural, socioeconomic, and educational milieu. Yet they are generally unaware that their experience is not universal, and that their expectations and interpretations regarding their own and others' actions may differ significantly from those they are meeting in the university setting. The same may be said for the professors and college administrators whom these students meet, because the majority of students they have worked with in previous years have had cultural and socioeconomic backgrounds similar to theirs. Most professors do not share with New Majority students the experience of truly living on the edge financially, or living in a low-income neighborhood and attending its schools, or having no one within their circle of family or close friends who has successfully completed a university degree.

Let's look at one more example of how subliminal programming is operative every day, without our being aware of it. Consider the case of a science faculty member, Professor Smith, who has worked successfully with a student, Paul, as a research assistant over several years, so that they understand and respect each other in their respective roles. They have established a level of shared understanding that normally allows them to communicate accurately with each other, even if very cryptically when needed. On a particular day, Professor Smith is entertaining in his office an unexpected visiting academic from a university with a highly regarded science program in Professor Smith's discipline. Student Paul suddenly appears in the office doorway about to walk in, as he usually does every day at this time to check in. However, at this moment, the professor does not want to interrupt his visit with the guest, so the professor looks up at Paul, makes a slight movement of his head and eyes that communicates to Paul not to interrupt or enter the room. Paul easily "reads" what the professor is communicating, and backs out the door quickly and quietly, not feeling in the least that he is being rejected or put down by the professor, but rather feeling trusted and respected in being communicated with in this way. A "communication match," which depended upon a significant amount of shared subliminal behavior expectations, has occurred, allowing Professor Smith to continue talking with his important guest without interruption while at the same time not offending Paul. However, if Paul had been new to Professor Smith's class and lab, Paul would probably not have understood the professor's eye and head movements and may have blundered into awkwardly interrupting the two academics' conversation. Even if Paul had correctly "read" the subtle head and eye gestures, he would have retreated feeling embarrassed, undervalued, or even offended.

Why did a "communication match" happen so smoothly for Professor Smith and Paul? Because their interactions over the previous three years allowed Paul to gain a clear understanding that "it is important to Professor Smith to visit with any science professors from other institutions who happen to come by" and that "he never sends me away just because he doesn't want to see me." At this stage of their working relationship, they have come to share a whole set of operational, unarticulated, common understandings on several levels, their own "microculture." On the deepest level, they have basically agreed to maintain a positive working relationship with each other. At another level they share an assumption that it is important to maintain a friendly environment for visitors, especially visiting science academics. There are probably many other shared assumptions about visitors and a friendly office environment regarding such details as the time of day that this is occurring in relation to other activities under way at that time. A third level of shared meaning depends upon the "coding" that is embedded in the professor's eye movement and the slight "no" head movement. Over many months of working together, Paul has learned to interpret these nonverbal communication clues as telling him that "I'm not saying anything verbally but please read the rest of my body language." The slight nod of the head and quick eye movement also say, "This is an important visitor; please don't interrupt right now but I will be happy to see you later." Paul is able to read his professor's encoded messages accurately, withdrawing from the doorway without feeling insulted or ignored. They share a subliminal microculture.

The stories above clearly create a mental picture of what we mean by a communication mismatch and by a communication match. I've shared these examples so you will have a context in which to analyze the insights in the coming chapters. This concept provides a mindset for understanding what New Majority students are thinking as they try to navigate their new world of the college classroom, and how professors are often genuinely perplexed by their inability to get these students to respond as expected.

One more question about this phenomenon may remain. How does the idea of a communication mismatch differ from the much more commonly mentioned concept of *miscommunicating*? A miscommunication normally refers to a case in which the person who is trying to communicate has made some error in the words she used which results in her audience being misinformed or misunderstanding her intended meaning. Someone who has miscommunicated may identify the problem herself by saying, "Sorry, I misspoke," referring to an objective error, such as giving the room number as 732 when it is actually 372, or confusing two similar sounding words such as the countries of Zambia and Zanzibar. In these cases, the speaker either did not know the correct information or did not realize she was using incorrect words. A miscommunication can also happen when the speaker does not give a sufficiently complete explanation to communicate the intended idea, so listeners are confused or draw incorrect conclusions from the information given. If the speaker who is giving a talk concludes by saying, "The following event is in the next building over there" (pointing), but there are actually two buildings in that direction, someone who ends up in the wrong place can rightly say that there was a miscommunication about the correct location.

It could be said that in one sense a communication mismatch is one type of miscommunication. But there are many types of miscommunication that are not mismatches. Communication mismatches, and the difficult situations that result from them, refer only to circumstances where a person's communication is accurate in expressing her own thinking or feeling; no "misspeaking" occurs. Everyone who shares her background or context understands a meaning very similar to the speaker's intended message. However, for recipients of the message who don't share her background or context, the communication has a different and often unfortunate meaning that she did not intend. This is why it is a communication mismatch.

WATCHING FOR COMMUNICATION MISMATCH

Now that we have described the basic idea of what communication mismatch is, we can begin to explore how it illuminates some of the unproductive and otherwise baffling reactions of New Majority students in various classroom settings. The phenomenon of communication mismatches recognizes that both professors and students share the reality with all human beings that they are subconsciously influenced by the sociocultural milieu in which they grew up and also the milieu in which they currently live. This internal programming means that both professors and students have subtle and just-below-consciousness, semiautomatic response patterns that they fully expect are appropriate to the specific setting in which they are interacting. As college classrooms are filling up with New Majority students, it is more crucial than ever that professors become aware that these subtle response patterns and expectations exist in everyone, in themselves and in their students, and may come into play at any time.

We've seen above the examples related to a person's use of eye contact and how the person being communicated with automatically reads certain meanings into that mode of expression. If the professor and the student have different meanings attached to a behavior and neither of them realizes that their interpretations differ, it is highly likely that either the student will misunderstand what the professor is trying to communicate, or the professor will miss the intended meaning of what the student is trying to communicate.

Eye contact is only one of numerous verbal and nonverbal communication practices that can be involved in a communication mismatch between professors and their students. Another common example is whether a student believes it is appropriate and respectful to ask a question or to volunteer information if not personally and directly asked for it. Silence that appears to a professor as ignorance, noninterest, being unprepared, or even sullenness may not have that meaning at all for the student who is just behaving as family and community socialization have taught him. Another example is how close speakers stand to the person with whom they are speaking; this differs in various cultures and families, and the proximity may also carry various messages. Standing too close by one person's standards may mean that you are trying to impose your thoughts or dominate the other. On the other hand, standing farther away in some cultures is the polite thing to do when addressing someone more important such as your professor. In other sociocultural upbringings, perhaps including the professor's, standing that far away means the person lacks interest in the subject or wants to leave the conversation as soon as possible. Still another example is whether it is polite when you speak to someone to stand directly facing the person, or to turn slightly sideways so your face is actually pointing to the side of the person rather than directly toward the other's chest; this difference in stance has positive or negative meaning in some cultures and it is totally unnoticed and inconsequential in others.

Another tricky difference in subliminal expectations is the micropause between when one person finishes saying something and the appropriate moment for the other person to begin responding. If a student is from a culture where they habitually wait a bit longer, maybe a full second, before answering, as some Alaska Native and Native Americans have subliminally learned from their elders, this can create a subliminal conundrum for the professor. The professor may be from a culture where speech happens very quickly or even overlaps from one speaker to the next with virtually no silence in between, as for instance some New Yorkers prefer to do. Or the professor may be from a culture where less than a half second is the normal wait before responding. When the student does not respond according to the timing that the professor subliminally expects, the professor may say another sentence to avoid what appears to him as an awkward silence. The student may leave a conversation with this professor having never said anything except in answer to a direct question, and may now believe that the professor didn't want to hear what the student had to say, because the professor never left enough time for the student to respond according to his built-in timer for responding. At the same time, the professor is trying to decide if the student is just not very smart or perhaps is shy, when neither of these characteristics is true.[8]

Yet another example is whether you have learned that it is acceptable and expected in a group meeting to speak up and share your opinion, or whether you should not do so until and unless someone directly calls on you or asks for your opinion, even when you have a definite view to share. Professors who become aware of this subliminal norm in some Asian American and Native American students have learned to directly ask those students, by name, for their opinions at some appropriate time in the discussion, and have thus avoided communication mismatch.[9]

Examples of differences in subliminal communication rules and expectations could go on and on, but these few demonstrate how well-meaning professors can misinterpret New Majority students' communications and therefore be unable to give the positive encouragement they intend to share. To prevent these unfortunate circumstances, it is important that professors work at becoming more conscious of their own subliminal communication habits and also work to acquire greater skill at perceiving when a mismatch with a student might be happening.

The Breakthrough Strategies presented in the following chapters are built on the premise that with increased awareness of subliminal factors at work within oneself as well as those belonging to one's students, it becomes more possible to be effective in guiding and successfully motivating New Majority students. As you read these chapters, your understanding of the concept of communication mismatch will become more robust, thereby creating an expanded basis for analyzing your own daily observations and giving you an increased understanding of what is happening in your classroom. It is my belief that by learning about these strategies, some of which you may choose to use, you will begin to see more possibilities for interacting with your New Majority students in ways that help them stretch to higher levels of academic achievement. You will then become able to make your own additional discoveries of strategies that are effective with New Majority students.

PART ONE

STRATEGIES FOR ENGAGEMENT

ENGAGED LEARNING is a very widely recognized and talked-about characteristic necessary for student success, and the reader has undoubtedly heard this phrase many times. Most college professors will recognize two types of students they frequently see: the minimally engaged students, and the alert, focused ones. The route to turning all or almost all students into engaged learners must entail ways to increase both their concentration level for enhanced intellectual participation and their emotional involvement for genuine interest and motivation. Strategies that result in increases in *both* concentration *and* interest or motivation are the most helpful in achieving engaged learning. This section introduces three strategies that have proven to be helpful in engaging New Majority students in college classrooms: effective feedback, help with questioning, and the creative use of analogies.

CHAPTER 4

Engaging Students Through Effective Feedback

PROFESSOR SMITH SHOOK HER HEAD as she looked at the next student paper in the pile she was correcting for her Nutrition Science class. These papers were supposed to be a revision of the students' earlier drafts. But this student certainly hadn't taken that task seriously!

The assignment started out as a paper the students wrote as a response to a presentation by a guest speaker two weeks earlier. Professor Smith had carefully reviewed each paper, writing comments, suggestions, and corrections on the initial drafts. She had returned the papers and explained the next assignment: "Read the comments on your paper and use them to prepare a second draft. When you finish the second draft, staple your first draft behind your new one and hand them in together. That way I can see if you really responded to my comments."

But now she was looking at Frank's paper. He hadn't written a second draft, but only handed in his first draft paper again, with this scrawled across the top of the paper: "Sorry. I can't do any better than this. But thanks for your not [note]." An arrow was drawn to the bottom of the page where her note was written.

Professor Smith was mystified. Why hadn't Frank written a revision of his paper? She looked again at the comment she had written under Frank's last paragraph. She remembered clearly her thought process in writing it. Since Frank was one of only a handful of African Americans in her class, and obviously a first-gen student from comments he had made during class discussions, she had deliberately tried to say something encouraging in her end-of-paper comment. She read it again. It said, "Good start, Frank. I'm sure your next draft will be very good." Like other student papers, she had also circled a number of grammar and spelling errors in red throughout the paper. "I certainly gave him positive feedback to develop confidence so he would write a good revision. What more could I do?" Feeling exasperated and at a dead end, Professor Smith laid aside Frank's paper, planning to ask him about it the next day.

As Frank entered the classroom the following afternoon, Professor Smith motioned him over to her desk. She had his paper in her hand and asked: "Frank, why didn't you do the revision, as you were asked?" Frank looked down and said, "I just didn't think I could do anything better." Professor Smith was baffled and just shook her head. "Well, I thought you could, or I wouldn't have written that note at the bottom of your first draft." That seemed to catch Frank's attention, and he looked up quizzically. "You did?" An awkward silence ensued, and when Professor Smith glanced up at the classroom clock—which showed that it was time to start the class—Frank looked down again and mumbled, "Well, I better sit down so you can start the class," and walked to his seat toward the back of the room.

WHAT'S GOING ON HERE?

On a first reading of this story, experienced professors may conclude that Frank is simply not a very highly motivated student or perhaps he lacks the necessary confidence. What is mystifying is why the encouraging comment from his professor, who is white, did not give him the extra boost of confidence or motivation he needed to prepare a second draft of the paper. A key piece of information in this student-professor story is the fact that Frank is not only a first-gen student but also in this class a minority, one of only a handful of African American students.

This reality is important because it tunes us into the issue of how the student is seeing his identity.

In the classroom, as in every setting we encounter in our lives, various aspects of who we are play a role in how we see ourselves and how others see us in that environment. These identity factors might include obvious things like height, weight, clothing, language, ethnicity, gender, age, and physical ableness. They might also include less obvious factors like family background, income level, athletic abilities, educational level, marital status, and religious affiliation. Each one of us carries a number of these factors as part of our identities. Whether one of those facets is especially noticeable to me at a specific time and place depends upon whether or not that particular aspect of my identity is important for how I will function in this setting. For instance, when I attend a regional conference of college professors, I am not paying much attention to the fact that I am a woman. The attendees are both men and women and neither gender is obviously in the majority. But when I first became a college president, I was the only woman president of a four-year college or university in the state of Washington. So when I attended a meeting of presidents for the state, I was highly aware of being the only woman, even if I tried not to dwell on this reality. When Frank walked into Professor Smith's classroom at the beginning of the term, Frank's awareness of his identity as an African American was significantly heightened. When he looked around the room he realized that most of the other students and the professor were not African American. Could this fact help Professor Smith understand Frank's response?

Yes. A relevant concept from social psychology—stereotype threat—sheds some light on our questions. In simple terms, a person experiences stereotype threat when he enters a setting where he knows that some people, particularly the type of people in this setting, have a negative stereotype regarding one facet of his identity. Knowing that the people he is now with may be negatively stereotyping him triggers a sense of heightened vigilance and pressure to demonstrate that this bad stereotype is not true of him. When a person feels this tension, he is experiencing stereotype threat. This concept is explained brilliantly and very readably in a book by Claude M. Steele, a social psychologist and formerly the executive vice chancellor and provost at the University of California, Berkeley. Here's how Steele describes this concept from social psychology.

> I believe stereotype threat is a standard predicament of life. It springs from our human powers of intersubjectivity—the fact that as members of society we have a pretty good idea of what other members of our society think about lots of things, including the major groups and identities in society. We could all take out a piece of paper, write down the major stereotypes of these identities, and show a high degree of agreement in what we wrote. That means that whenever we're in a situation where a bad stereotype about one of our own identities could be applied to us—such as those about being old, poor, rich, or female—we know it. We know what "people could think." We know that anything we do that fits the stereotype could be taken as confirming it. And we know that, for that reason, we could be judged and treated accordingly . . . It is present in any situation to which the stereotype is relevant. And this means that it follows members of the stereotyped group into these situations like a balloon over their heads.[1]

Frank's identity as an African American is relevant in this setting, because our society, including academia, has the stereotype that African Americans on average aren't as smart in school and university academic work. In reality, Frank is a competent student who has performed adequately so far in his university career. But knowing the stereotype that both his teacher and his classmates undoubtedly have about people like him in academic settings, he will feel extra pressure to show his professor that in fact he is a competent student. This makes him feel uneasy, on guard to disprove the negative stereotype, and therefore a bit threatened. The chances are good that he is experiencing a classic stereotype threat in this class, and that it may be affecting the way he responded to the directive to revise his paper.

Understanding stereotype threat can be very insightful for professors, because there are many ways in which stereotype threats may arise in academic settings. Students from ethnicities or nationalities that are stereotyped as poor achievers in scholastic endeavors will feel some amount of stereotype threat as they join any class. Women will also have to deal with stereotype threat when they decide to major in computer science or mathematics. Men will have the same challenge when they choose to major in nursing. White men joining a college's track and field program with black athletes will feel a stereotype threat every time they step up to the starting line with their African American peers. First-gen students attending a university where most of the students are from college-going families experience stereotype threat as their status as first-gen university students becomes evident. Most of them are also low-income, and this additional factor, which may become evident through the nonstandard English they use in conversation, or through the clothing they wear, or through the topics of their conversations, will heighten the stereotype pressure. This will happen because another common stereotype of our American culture is that low-income people aren't as smart as professional and middle-class folks; if they were, they would have gotten themselves out of poverty.

Given all the opportunities for stereotype threat to become operative among New Majority students, research has shown some of the practical effects of stereotype threats on university students, regardless of which stereotype threat they are facing. Basically, being in a setting where a negative stereotype is operative relative to some aspect of your identity inevitably causes you increased tension and pressure. You may only be minimally aware of this, because you are concentrating on being successful in that setting. But in actuality you are subliminally being affected by your awareness that some of those around you have negative expectations of your ability to perform, based on some aspect of your identity. The fact that this actually happens has been verified in numerous research settings, both by interviewing participants and by measuring such things as blood pressure and heart rate, which almost always rise significantly as stereotype threat is experienced.[2] More important, research has also shown that actual performance is being negatively affected by the stereotype threat, whether the person is aware of that causal connection or not.[3] One way to understand this is that your brain is being distracted from full attention on the task before you with the periodic mental interruption, "They don't think I can do this," and then, "I have to show them" or "and I'm not really sure if I can do this. They might be right." Brain science has told us that being distracted from a challenging task, switching back and forth between the task and something else, compromises the effectiveness of whatever our brains are trying to achieve.[4] So it is not surprising that when a student is in a setting that evokes a stereotype threat, the results of the student's academic task effort will be less than ideal.

Applying these insights to the scenario between Professor Smith and Frank allows us to see that there is a high probability that Frank is dealing with stereotype threat as he tries to function effectively in this class. Just being in an academic setting in which he is a minority African American, and having a white professor, may immediately trigger his awareness that others around him must be wondering if he is up to the challenge of the class. That's the stereotype that Frank knows is out there. However, as we see the note that Professor Smith put on Frank's paper and hear her comment that she believes Frank could write a good follow-up paper, we can conclude that that professor was deliberately trying to counteract any lack of confidence which Frank might have. But it didn't seem to work.

FEEDBACK TO COUNTER STEREOTYPE THREAT

The challenge is how a professor or mentor can give effective feedback that will simultaneously fill two needs. On the one hand, the professor needs to push students to go beyond their initial level of work. They need to be challenged to go deeper, think harder, and be more comprehensive or more detailed or more accurate. On the other hand, the professor wants to encourage and support students who may be susceptible to stereotype threat because of their ethnicity, educational background, or socioeconomic status. Their lack of confidence needs to be shored up. How can professors meet these two apparently contradictory needs? Geoff Cohen, Claude Steele, and Lee Ross conducted some amazing research at Stanford University with black and white students to test several potential answers to this dilemma. The experiments tested three different approaches to giving feedback to essays the students had written, followed by interviews with the students to find out how much they trusted the feedback and how motivated they were to improve their essays. The results were very instructive.

In the first approach, researchers were neutral about the quality of the essay and focused on giving suggested changes. In the second approach, researchers began by giving a positive encouraging statement, much like Professor Smith's notation on the bottom of Frank's paper, and they followed that with recommendations for the revision. The third way started with an explanation that high standards were being used in evaluating the essays, followed by an assurance that, having read the student's first draft, the reviewer was sure the student could meet those high standards, and ending with recommendations for the revision.

Students' responses to these three different approaches revealed that the third way was the only approach that consistently resulted in the black students saying they trusted the feedback at the same level that white students reported, and that it motivated them to improve their essays.[5] This third feedback model was, for black students, as Claude Steele said, "like water on parched land—something they rarely seemed to get, but that, once they got it, renewed their trust and ability to be motivated by the criticism."[6]

A relevant question regarding Professor Smith's dilemma is why the second type of feedback—giving positive encouraging comments to the student—did not work. The answer seems to be that just giving assurances to the student does not address the stereotype threat issue. A positive assurance, with no reference to what level of academic performance is the basis for the professor's judgment of student work, can be interpreted as actually affirming the negative stereotype. The student might well think, "She's just saying a positive comment because she doesn't think I can do any better and doesn't want me to feel bad." If a student is already experiencing some doubts about whether or not he really "is college material," then his thoughts will inevitably include, "Maybe the professor's doubts are right, that I can't do this level of work. She's probably right; I probably can't."

As professors attempt to understand stereotype threat that may be occurring in their own classrooms, it can be helpful for them to think back on their own experience, and see if they can recall a personal experience of stereotype threat. Perhaps a professor remembers participating in a sport in which he was shorter than the other players and keenly aware that others would be thinking he couldn't hold his own in the sport. Or perhaps another professor who is white remembers being a college student in a Latin American literature class where she was surprised to be the only white person among an entire class of Latino/as and how nervous she felt that she would be seen as insensitive or racist when the class discussions centered on critiquing a piece of literature. As I considered my own experiences, I thought more about the incident I referred to earlier. As a relatively new president, I remember attending a meeting with nine male college presidents as the only woman president among the ten private nonprofit colleges and universities in Washington State. At that time in the early 1980s only 10 percent of college presidents nationally were women.[7] I remember walking into the meeting room where many of the presidents were already seated around a large conference table. All of them instantly stood up, and two of them immediately stepped forward to pull out the chair for me at my place at the table. I was startled and I began asking myself: "They're trying so hard to be nice to me because I don't really fit here and they don't want me to feel bad." I'm usually a talkative, relaxed conversationalist, but with this all-male presidents group standing quietly as I tried to accept graciously the help (which I didn't need) with my chair, I found my mind racing. I was so sure they were thinking, "I wonder how much she knows about being a college president or if she is really up to speed on all our complex issues." The fact that they were being ceremoniously deferential to me, which I knew they had not done for each other, just increased my anxiety and muddled my thinking. I remember feeling my stomach tightening as I tried to focus my mind more acutely on how I could counter their presumptions about my lack of presidential know-how. As I remember now, I said very little during the meeting, and the few times I wanted to make a comment, my brain interrupted me by asking, "Are you sure this is really a cogent, relevant comment? If not, you better not say it." Stereotype threat was interrupting my normal good judgment, although I didn't know the term at the time. On campus I rarely felt incompetent or tongue-tied, but I was surprised that in this circumstance I definitely felt maybe I was not up to the task of being a college president, at least in the way the male presidents saw the job. This feeling was actually heightened by the gracious formal behavior of the other presidents as I joined them at the meeting, even though those male college presidents had the best of intentions.

In revisiting this unsettling experience in my mind, I realize that it is very relevant to the challenge facing professors who are trying to encourage New Majority students. It is certainly possible to inadvertently exacerbate stereotype threat feelings that students may be experiencing when some aspect of their identity connected with a stereotype of incompetence, such as low-income level, ethnicity, or lack of college-educated family, becomes evident. While my male president colleagues were aware of the general stereotype that women are not equipped to be successful leaders in universities and large corporations, they were consciously trying to give me the "benefit of the doubt." They just didn't know that their over-the-top graciousness and courteous behavior actually had the opposite effect. If I apply the significant elements in my story to the second approach for giving feedback that the Stanford students experienced, it is evident why giving only praise and encouragement is ineffective in countering a stereotype threat.

The third feedback method calls for combining an assuring statement with a clear and strong statement about high standards. It rules out for the student the possibility that the professor's supportive comment is made just to make the student feel good even though the professor doubts that the student is competent. And that immediately lessens the stress of the stereotype threat.

At Heritage University, we approached Professor Mary James, associate dean of arts and sciences, who had been identified by the student researchers as someone who was very successful in helping students improve their writing. Our research in the literature had acquainted us with the experiment at Stanford University, and we shared that with Professor James. Remarkably, she was already doing something quite similar, although she had not heard about the Stanford experiment and its relation to stereotype threat. She immediately decided to alter her approach a bit to use the system detailed in this study.[8] When she met individually with her students about their writing, she carefully followed a one-two-three plan in giving feedback. First, she told the student that she had very high standards for acceptable essays and written projects and she always stuck to this standard. Then she said that she was convinced that this specific student could meet those standards, having read the work produced so far or observed the student's participation in class. Thirdly, she went over the specific changes and improvements she suggested for the paper's revision. The results were encouraging, as she began to see more students produce a new draft of the paper that was actually a significant improvement. Professor James's approach effectively deflates students' worries about a negative stereotype based on their group's intellectual abilities. With that worry out of the way, students' natural motivation can rise to the top and their energy can focus one hundred percent on improved performance.

Over time, Professor James added a fourth step. At the end of the feedback session, she asked the student to estimate when they would complete the revision of the paper and to make an appointment right then for bringing the revised paper back to her. She entered the appointment in her calendar as the student entered it in his or hers. Lastly she asked students for a cell phone number that she could use if they did not keep the appointment. This fourth step, providing a concrete follow-up plan for the student, gave yet another boost to the positive results of her feedback process. By securing a commitment from students that they would indeed work on a revision of their project or paper because they now had a concrete date and time to report back, more students actually revised their papers in a meaningful way than had done so previously. These four steps resulted in students' serious commitments to improving their writing, and the essays they produced were a confirmation of the method's effectiveness.

GIVING EFFECTIVE FEEDBACK

In short, an effective feedback strategy has the following four steps:

1. Make a firm statement about the high standards you always use in assessing any student's work.

2. State your belief that based on previous work or accomplishments of this student you are convinced the student can meet your high standards.
3. Give specific recommendations for improving the project or writing.
4. Ask the student to make an appointment now for a specific day and time to bring the revised paper or project back to you.

More generally, there are several other proven techniques that professors can use to help students counter the effects of stereotype threat. These include increasing students' awareness of how stereotype threat might be affecting their work in the first place, as well as encouraging them to use the kind of study methods that their continuing-generation classmates are probably already using, especially the practice of group study.

Addressing Stereotype Threat Directly

In situations where professors believe that the issue of stereotype threat may be impacting a number of students in a given class, it may be useful to take time to introduce students to this phenomenon so that their own recognition of it in themselves may lessen the tension and distraction that they experience. One method would be to assign a reading on stereotype threat and conduct a class discussion to help students absorb and apply the concept to their own lives.

Another approach is through the professor's personal story-telling. This can be done just before the professor returns papers with written feedback on them, as a way to pre-program students to take seriously the revisions suggested. An engaging way to use story-telling is for the professor to recall and retell an experience of stereotype threat that he or she has experienced, with all the detail that a good story includes. Reviewing your experiences in such areas as sports participation, cross-cultural travel, attending special extraordinary events, or various academic settings, may help you identify a good personal example or perhaps one you heard about from a family member. As you tell the story to the class, it is especially important to include information on how your performance was compromised because of experiencing the mental and emotional disruption of stereotype threat. As I related above, that is what I experienced during my meeting with the all-male college presidents group, but I only realized later that I had not contributed insights or intelligent comments at the meeting as I usually did.

Encouraging Study Groups

Some years ago Philip Uri Treisman carried out a very telling research effort. He decided to deepen the learning and study behavior of his African American mathematics students at Berkeley who were not performing as well in his calculus class as their SAT scores had predicted. What he discovered was that his very successful Asian students spent a good deal of their math study time working together in groups on assignments, helping each other understand how to derive the answers. His white students also spent some time studying together, but more often they contacted tutors and spent time with them. However, his African American students studied in isolation and when quizzed about this, it became evident that it had to do with the stereotype they knew was out there that said they were less competent in difficult subjects like calculus. They felt desperately driven to disprove this, and so they were afraid if they joined a study group with other students or consulted tutors, they might inadvertently be verifying the stereotype. They were therefore not benefiting from the group study that helped his Asian American and white students do better in solving the calculus problems. So he developed a new way of running his higher math classes that was built on group learning; he showed that this approach removed much of the mystifying low performance of high-SAT-scoring black students.[9]

This result is congruent with the more recent findings about the higher value that students from working-class and many nonwhite cultures place on community and interdependence rather than independence.[10] It is also a practical approach to counteracting students' identity threat reactions in challenging courses. Treisman designed group work that was integral to how he ran his classes, so students had to be involved. This is an approach that any professor who is teaching a challenging course in her subject can implement. To counteract the potential dangers of stereotype threat for her students from ethnic or socioeconomic groups with few representatives in her professional field, the professor can incorporate group learning opportunities that have a high potential for increasing the success rates of New Majority students. It is important that the group learning settings be carefully designed to require everyone to participate in their groups and to experience this opportunity often enough to facilitate student bonding and a sense of shared responsibility for everyone's learning.

SUMMARY

Thanks to the insights that social psychology provides to us about the subtle yet potentially harmful reality of stereotype threat, professors can now be much more confident that they are providing effective feedback to students on their papers and projects. By designing small study groups, professors can also provide a setting in which students can learn more easily or more in depth, while at the same time helping them deal with any stereotype threat worries that keep them from interacting candidly with their classmates. Using the feedback protocol or incorporating small study groups in the course requirements, as described above, and helping students recognize stereotype threat possibilities in their own lives, will motivate more students to greater academic achievement.

CHAPTER 5

Helping Students Ask Questions

CARMEN LOOKED WORRIED when I caught up with her as she walked across the campus. Her arms were loaded down with her backpack, books sticking out of the pocket. "How's it going?" I inquired casually. "Well, not too good," was her quiet answer. "What's not going well?" I probed. "I just don't understand some of those ideas Professor Johnson has been telling us. I'm listening real hard but I just don't get it." "Well, I'm sure you're asking questions, when he says something you don't understand," was my response, hoping to give an upbeat impetus to our conversation.

There was no response from Carmen. I glanced over at her and saw she was looking at the ground and not at me as she had been a minute ago. "You do ask questions, don't you, Carmen?" "No, I don't." "Why not? It's important." More silence, and then a firm answer: "My father always told me, 'Don't ask questions in public—you'll just look stupid.'"

I was stunned. A scene flashed into my mind from my childhood when my dad would tell us to think up good questions to ask our teachers. "If you ask good, strong questions, the teacher will think you are smart." And Dad modeled that attitude daily by asking what we had learned that day in school and encouraging conversation that helped us formulate further inquiry into the day's new ideas, including lots of questions.

Looking at Carmen's determined face, it was evident that she was convinced it wasn't a good idea to ask questions. I tried to punch a little hole in that conviction: "Well, I don't think you would look stupid, Carmen." But her response was immediate: "None of my friends ask questions, and I know they'd think I looked dumb if I did."

So I tried a different tack. "Well, you could wait in the room after class, and when the other students have left the room, you could then go up to ask Professor Johnson your question when no one else is around, and I know he would help you understand." Carmen responded right away. "I tried that, but Professor Johnson likes to walk out of class with the last group of students leaving. He likes to walk across campus with them, so I never have a chance to talk to him."

WHAT'S GOING ON HERE?

My conversation with this worried student alerted me to a problem I did not know existed. Yes, I knew that any student from any background can be afraid of asking "dumb questions." Each of us remembers at least one time being a student in a class with an intimidating teacher. We remember having thought about trying not to ask "dumb questions." But Carmen's story raised an entirely new set of concerns. In the weeks following this conversation with Carmen, I asked several other students on the Heritage University campus if they had ever been given any direction from their parents about asking questions. Universally, they answered, "Oh yes! 'Don't ask questions in public' was what I was always told." The reason given for not asking questions differed slightly across individual responses: "because you'll just look stupid," or "especially if the person is more important than you," or "if it's a person you're supposed to have respect for," or "you're supposed to figure things out by watching and listening; you should learn answers from observing," or "we don't ask questions in public—it's not our way." The contrast between this strongly held conviction and my clear memory of being told it was smart to think up good questions created a haunting concern about how these students, coming from a "no-questions-in-public" milieu, would be able to function effectively in academia where asking questions as part of classroom dialogue is key to the processing of new information. I was also asking myself how these students would get help when they needed to ask a professor before or after class a question central to correctly completing an assignment. As I thought about my own undergraduate experience, I couldn't remember a class in which I had not asked the professor a question or advice outside of the general class session. Stopping at his or her desk before or after class helped me with such concerns as how to focus my writing project or where to find elusive research information or how to identify the most important topics to study before a difficult test. Revisiting my own memories made me feel the urgency of addressing this "no questions" mindset. I concluded that it is vitally important for faculty to make it explicit to students why they need to push themselves to ask questions even though it might go against their cultural norms. These reasons include:

- You don't really understand a new concept or fact unless you can relate it to other things you already know, and when you do that, there are normally questions that arise about the new idea in relation to other known areas.
- Our brains find it much easier to remember and understand new information if we not only hear it but start speaking about it; when you try to develop questions about the new idea, you have to talk about it, thus helping your brain to remember the new idea.
- College-level learning seeks to develop persons who not only know many facts, but who are also independent, critical thinkers; this requires you to consider if a new idea makes sense in light of what else you already know.

Most of us professors working with Heritage University's Institute for Student Identity and Success are from families where the generation before us had some college-degree holders. We can remember stories we heard about family members' college experiences that included asking questions during class, or quizzing a professor outside of class. Moreover, our white middle-class backgrounds posited as a norm that it was good to ask intelligent questions, to participate in discussions with queries as well as comments, because it showed that you were interested in others and what they are saying. As children we were praised for this behavior. Most of us remember that if we didn't have anything to say as young people during a conversation with adults, we would be asked later, "Are you feeling okay?" because we were so quiet. In contrast, we were observing that many of the Heritage students from immigrant families had learned a different norm. When they were with elders or people more important than they, it was not considered respectful to speak up or ask questions. Just listening attentively was the appropriate response.

It was something new for us to hear students sharing the advice they had received: "Never ask questions because you'll just look stupid." It would be one thing to be encouraged to ask good questions, or be told to think something through carefully before asking a question. But to be warned never to ask questions in front of others? We began to analyze how such a directive would shape the mental mindset that a student brings to a college classroom. We thought about the various implications and consequences of this mindset. It became evident that this mindset would have a significant influence both on the external non-questioning behavior of students and on the internal mental processes they would employ during class: students would be focusing on absorbing and recording information being shared by the professor or presenter rather than on actively engaging with the information, questioning aspects that were unclear or perplexing. Very little critical thinking would be happening. This would also influence the behavior of the professor. On reflection, it also appears that this is one of those subliminal differences in internal norms of behavior which very infrequently rise to a conscious level. Neither those whose subliminal norm is "it's good to ask questions" nor those whose subliminal programming says "never ask questions of someone more important than you, especially in front of others," are consciously aware of this behavior norm. It's just what you do. It's how you naturally approach situations. And you don't know that some of your fellow human beings are programmed with quite a different norm in regard to question-asking. For both professors and students, bringing these two contradictory norms to full consciousness and looking at the implications of them can be a very valuable exercise.

As we studied this phenomenon, we began to envision some of the implications that might play out for the professor who is unaware that most of the students in a classroom were from homes where the "don't ask questions" instruction was the norm. We imagined a professor in a modest-sized classroom, presenting a complex new idea, explaining it as carefully as she could for opening this topic, and ending her presentation with the sincere query, "What questions do you have about this concept?" Students who have been looking at her and watching the screen at the front of the room intently throughout the presentation suddenly stop looking at the professor and look down. No one raises a hand. No one speaks up. So the professor says, "Was that all clear to everyone? Do you understand this concept?" Some nod their heads in a sort of tentative fashion with their eyes looking off to the corner of the room. Others just avert their eyes. Silence reigns. Obviously, the reality that is unfolding before the professor does not match what her presumption had been as she prepared for this class. She expected that she would have to explain again or perhaps in different ways some of the more complex aspects of today's concept, or its implications for other areas of the subject matter. The silence and nonresponsiveness are unexpected.

Various professors may react to this scenario in different ways. One may feel that students are distancing themselves from her, that they are not comfortable with her, even though she has made every effort in preparing this lecture to put this new concept in easy-to-follow language, complete with diagrams and visuals. "Maybe I failed in my goal for today, I just didn't present this topic adequately, but no one is willing to tell me." This reaction in the mind of the professor reinforces and heightens the feeling of heaviness in the room, and that creates a communication dead space.

Or the professor may surmise that these students didn't read the assigned chapter on this topic, as she had requested, and so they would have had difficulty in following the presentation today, and don't want to own up to not preparing for the class. This thought would lead quickly to a growing conviction in the mind of the professor that these students don't really have any interest in this subject, that they are certainly not prime candidates to major in her discipline. Any additional effort to reach them might even be a waste of time. With these thoughts racing through the mind of the professor, she may well stop looking out at the students, step back to the desk, or start organizing her lecture notes. The students sense a gulf developing between themselves and the professor. Students may already be thinking, "See, she doesn't really understand us." Or, "She doesn't really think we can get this." Or, "I don't really get this, but I guess that's just the way it is."

It is evident from these likely scenarios with New Majority students that there is a major mismatch between the professor's mindset about students' questions ("If they are listening, if they are interested, and if they are prepared, they will ask me questions."), and the students' mindset about asking questions ("I would never ask a question in front of the other students, and especially to someone more important. I've always been taught that's really a stupid thing to do.") Moreover, this fairly simple communication mismatch can easily play out in a much more complex and troublesome deterioration of the faculty-student relationship. It can undermine the confidence level and therefore the commitment to persevere on the part of students. In short, it is very important that the faculty member take action early on to turn this potential minefield into an opportunity for greater understanding between a professor and her students, and to lead students into greater engagement in the learning process.

CONFRONTING THE PROBLEM

To find ways to address this issue, I turned to the work our research assistants were doing. Based on the anonymous oral survey answers they were gathering, we picked out the names of several professors who were mentioned as "being easy to talk to" and "easy to ask him/her questions." Then I followed up with several in-depth interviews with professors who had been named by students as especially effective. The purpose of the interviews was to discover some key strategies that could be used to deal with the "don't ask questions" syndrome.

Interviewing several professors about how they got students to engage in questioning during class was very revealing. It became obvious that professors who had very consciously reflected on the non-question-asking behavior of their students were also the ones who had come to recognize the presence of subliminal norms on this topic, although they didn't necessarily name it as such. While I had only recently become aware of the hidden dictum "don't ask questions; you'll just look stupid," thanks to my conversation with Carmen, these professors had already bumped into this reality previously. They explained in various ways that, on reflection, they had become aware that their presumption that "it's good to ask questions so you can understand better," differed substantially from the mindset of their New Majority students. Gradually these professors had become convinced that their students were not just especially shy or afraid of asking an especially dumb-sounding question. Rather, it became clear that the norm among the students was not to ask questions, period. Even if you are encouraged to do so. When I asked the professors if they had heard students say that their parents or other family authority figures had told them never to ask questions in public, one said yes, and the others said they had surmised as much from the widespread similar behavior by most of their students. "I figured out pretty quickly that asking questions in a college class was just something these students think you don't do," said one professor. "It became obvious to me that they didn't know that some of their fellow human beings, including their professors, had different expectations and experiences with regard to question-asking during classes." As the interviews proceeded and I probed for specific strategies that professors used, I observed that it made a big difference if a professor had a conscious recognition of the differing unspoken, contradictory behavior norms regarding question-asking between faculty and their New Majority students. When professors brought these two contradictory norms to full consciousness and looked at the implications of them, creative solutions began to emerge. They were the professors who had great suggestions to share.

STRATEGIES TO ENCOURAGE QUESTIONS

Here are some useful ideas that surfaced during interviews with faculty. Professors can employ one or several of these ideas in a given class. Some approaches may be more appropriate than others for certain subject areas.

Reframe the Role of the Professor

The student's presumption that she will "look stupid if I ask a question" is based on the preconception she has of the faculty member as a person with much higher status than she has, someone who has not only more knowledge but also more social respect and therefore should be treated with great deference. One Heritage University faculty member, Michael Parra, assistant professor of biochemistry, has developed an approach that he uses to counteract this exaggerated silent veneration from students. At the outset of the course, he clearly describes himself as the students' "guide"—not the students' "grade-giver." "I don't give grades," he says emphatically to students. "You give yourself a grade by how hard you work, and by how much mastery you achieve with the course material and the requirements in the syllabus. I'm just your guide. You tell me how hard you want to work, and I'll match that as your guide." By repeating this statement periodically, which students find surprising and countercultural to their upbringing, Professor Parra begins to chip away at the pedestal on which students automatically place him. Another approach to changing the students' image of the professor as an intimidating, more important person who deserves to be on a pedestal, is discussed as part of the "First Day" exercises suggested in chapter 7.

Have a Candid Discussion About Asking Questions

You can start this conversation with your class by simply asking students for their experiences. Here are several discussion starters:

- Have any of you had your parents or other adults tell you, "Don't ask questions; you'll just look stupid"?
- Can someone tell us a story about when you were given that advice? (If possible get several students to share their stories so the similarities and differences will emerge).
- Can someone share a story about a time or place when you really needed to ask a question, but you didn't because you were very aware of the advice not to ask questions?
- If you got advice not to ask questions, what effect did that advice have on you at the time? How did it affect your behavior? Does it still affect your behavior?

In a large class, these questions may spark more conversation if they are discussed in smaller groups, with some summary ideas reported back to the whole group afterward.

At some point, the professor should share his own experience learning about questioning behavior. Or he could quiz several of his colleagues about their experiences of learning to ask questions and share their experiences. One or more of these stories should demonstrate for students that many people in the world of academia learned as young people, and now operate from the presumption, that it is very acceptable and even highly admired to ask good questions. This will help New Majority students to understand why their professors seem to be frequently pressing the students to ask questions, even though students are obviously uncomfortable doing so. Point out that academics' way of thinking about questions is based on the assumption that you will ask questions politely and respectfully, and that questions are a very important way to not only learn more effectively and efficiently, but also to demonstrate that you were listening carefully, or that you understood something well enough to ask a follow-up question, or that you have become engaged in the topic enough to see implications and contradictions. Point out that you will judge the students' "class participation," listed as a requirement or a way to earn extra points in the syllabus, partially by observing how often they ask questions. You will be listening for questions that show they have been paying attention, or that demonstrate an awareness of the implications of a topic, or that illustrate that they are making connections with another topic previously studied in this or another class.

Whenever feasible, engaging the whole class in this conversation will open new insights for both the students and the faculty member. It will also set the stage for the professor to engage other strategies that will help students overcome their fear of asking questions.

Practice with Texts

Another initial strategy to encourage question-asking behavior at the beginning of a new class is to associate it with assigned readings of a chapter in the textbook or a professional article distributed to students. Professor Maria Cuevas at Yakima Valley Community College has developed this into a very effective strategy. After identifying the chapter or article that will be a reading assignment, she asks students to call out the headings and subheadings in the reading as she writes each of them on the board. She then invites students to form a team with two or three of the students sitting near them and then look carefully at the headings and subheadings on the board. Together they are to develop some questions that arise as they consider these headings. Examples she shares are questions such as "What does that word in the heading mean?" "What does the subheading have to do with the major heading it is under?" "Why did the author put that subheading there?" After a short time to develop their questions with their team, she calls the teams to the blackboard and has them write their questions beside each of the headings or subheadings. When they are finished, the board is covered with questions written at all angles next to the original headings, and Professor Cuevas comments on especially thoughtful questions and encourages student responses. When this exercise is finished, students then proceed to read the chapter or article, usually as homework, and they use the headings and subheadings as an outline for taking notes on the reading.

Professor Cuevas's exercise is meant primarily to engage students in thinking about the subject of the reading in a thoughtful way so they will really become engaged in it.[1] But the secondary outcome of this strategy is to give the students practice in posing questions. When I observed Professor Cuevas's class at the beginning of the term, it was obvious to me that the very reticent behavior that students began with was being transformed into lively efforts to come up with questions that were more interesting than their classmates'. After they have done this exercise several times with different readings, students are forming great habits of really grappling with the material they are going to read, and they are also overcoming their earlier restraint about asking questions.

Use Humor to Release Tension

To help students change their internal messaging system, which is programmed to tell them not to ask questions, and reprogram it to the exactly opposite behavior, requires a major transformation in the students' internal norm-dictating process. To change our behavior from long-practiced, comfortable conduct to a contradictory behavior is daunting for any of us. It makes us tense and anxious. Being tense and anxious, we have learned from neuroscience, tends to shut down the parts of our brains that can do higher-order thinking—like formulating a good, thoughtful question.[2] So it is important to find ways to help students overcome the anxiety they are experiencing as they practice a new skill of asking thoughtful questions. That is why using humor, briefly, but sprinkled liberally throughout the class time, is an excellent strategy. A good laugh immediately lowers the physical and mental tensions associated with doing something that you're not normally comfortable with.[3]

Any professor, even those who would not normally think of themselves as very humorous, can consciously adopt this strategy as part of the plan to build up the "good questioning" behavior of their students. There are several ways to go about this. If the faculty member is comfortable in telling jokes, she can begin keeping a file of ones that made her laugh and that relate, even obliquely, to the classroom setting or the topics studied. If the faculty member is not comfortable telling a joke, she can build up a collection of cartoons cut from the daily paper or from magazines like *The New Yorker* or the Sunday *Parade* magazine, scan them into the computer, and then throw one up on the screen in between topics during class. This is an easy practice to start, and while only utilizing a minute here or there throughout a class period, it can have a significant effect on empowering students to speak up and try out their questions. Of course, this strategy has to be used in concert with a process of engaging students in thinking of good questions and asking them.

Several of the professors I interviewed shared that they keep a list of good jokes they hear or read, and carefully choose one or two to share during each class. If they can choose one that relates to the topic for the day, they are especially happy. But if a joke related to the day's subject is not available, they can still choose one that will change the pace, reduce tension, and thereby encourage good thinking and good questions.

Use the "Think/Pair/Share" Method

This strategy is not unique to the goal of fostering good questions, and you may already be familiar with the general strategy from a faculty development session or materials from your university's teaching and learning center. This method is described very well in numerous websites and articles, such as one from Carleton College in Minnesota.[4] Essentially this is a formatted way to have students discuss material with one other student. In the case of this Breakthrough Strategy, Heritage's Professor Parra tweaked the Think/Pair/Share format from its usual use as a way to get students to come up with some good answers for the professor. Instead, he focuses it on getting the students to formulate good questions. It generally is a ten- to fifteen-minute exercise, used at the time in the class session when the professor wants to review and reinforce the material presented thus far, while encouraging students to develop good questions. Here's how to use it:

- The professor signals the beginning of the "Think" phase by posing a topic and instructing students: "Think about our topic (X) and what questions you might have about it. Your questions could be about the meaning of X, or they could be about how X applies to other situations or concepts, or how X interacts with other similar subjects, or any other questions you can think of. Please jot down your questions, so that you will be able to share them with your partner in a couple of minutes."
- After two or three minutes, the professor instructs students to pair with one other student nearby and share his or her questions with the other.
- After three to five minutes of the "Pairing" phase, the professor again gets the attention of the whole class and calls on random students to share their questions. He tells them, "You can share one of your own questions, or you can share one that your talking partner expressed."
- By making affirming comments about the questions as they are shared by students, the professor reinforces a positive, encouraging environment for asking questions. It is important to call on several students and hear their questions, focusing on why they are valid, good questions, before stopping to actually answer any of the questions posed.

The easy-to-remember name of this exercise, "Think/Pair/Share," may be familiar to some students who have been exposed to it in high school or other college classes. However, they have probably used the exercise to generate student comments rather than to formulate questions, so it may be necessary for the professor to explain carefully the purpose for this exercise before it starts, so students maintain the focus on coming up with good questions, not answers. This gives the professor a chance to reiterate why it is vital for students to become proficient in asking questions.

Reward Students Who Pose Exceptional Questions

Another clever way to develop an atmosphere where students are anxious to ask good questions, rather than being anxious not to ask questions, is to provide an incentive. Professor Parra tells students and puts in his syllabus, "If you can ask a meaningful question about the topic we're studying that the Professor can't answer, you will receive five extra points." The real value of this strategy is that it provides an immediate, concrete motivation for students to ask good questions. As the student mentally explores possible questions to ask, she can focus on having the opportunity to improve her grade by getting extra points, rather than on the gnawing worry of laying herself open to ridicule by asking a strange question.

There may be a few subject areas that require the professor to give a more nuanced explanation of what kind of questions can earn extra points, particularly if the subject would invite a great number of trivial questions that are not important for successfully mastering the subject. For instance, if the class is studying Shakespeare's plays, a student could ask a very trivial question about some minor detail that is unrelated to the essence of the plot or the character development or the deeper themes of the play. This is not the kind of questioning that the professor wants to foster by offering extra points. But if the professor defines at the outset a bit more fully what kind of questions will earn extra points, the strategy can be useful.

The professor must also be willing to be totally honest with students for this strategy to work, but most professors readily admit that there are many things about their subjects that they don't know or would have to look up. When a student asks such a question, Professor Parra responds that it is a good question and he does not know the answer. He then tells the student to try to find the answer before the next class and promises that he will do the same. When the student returns with an answer to the question, or at least evidence that he or she searched hard for an answer, the student's course point total increases by a specified number of points. Students definitely become more fully engaged when they are matching wits with their professor by thinking up a question he can't answer, but also getting a tangible reward toward a good grade.

ADDITIONAL FACULTY INSIGHTS

Having a class full of students who don't ask questions can be one of the most frustrating realities in the first weeks of a term. Professors have emphasized that it is very important to take action on this barrier to student success very soon after the class starts. If you wait too long, students are already comfortable with the non-questioning atmosphere of the class and assume that the instructor is also okay with it. So when the professor tries to change that behavior after several weeks of class, the students don't take the effort very seriously and it takes much longer to get them to change their behavior.

Some faculty have said that it is actually better, if you are teaching in an institution where you know that a significant number of your students are first-generation and low-income, to assume that you will have a problem with very low participation in questioning when you are planning your class. With this approach, you will plan to use one or more of the strategies described above right from the first class session. Don't wait until this behavior becomes evident in the classroom.

Another faculty insight is that it may be easier to get truly reticent students to begin asking questions if they can do it at first outside of the regular class time. This will happen if they can interact with the professor informally and become a little more comfortable in ordinary, casual conversation with the professor. Then they usually will be more responsive when the professor urges them in class to ask questions.[5] For instance, if you have given students an assignment that requires them to do some research in the library, you can hang out in the library near the area where students are likely to come. Or you can go to the cafeteria at a time when lots of students are there. By greeting them in a very friendly way when you see them in an informal setting, you may be able to engage them in small talk and gradually make inroads into their fear of asking you questions about material they don't understand, once they are back in class.

Another creative faculty member at Heritage University, Professor Sara Cartmel, shared her very up-front approach to the issue of encouraging students to feel free to speak with her. She adds the following to her syllabus for a freshman course: "Required: come to the professor's office during her office hours (which are listed below) a minimum of twice during the term." In fulfilling this simple requirement, the professor says that the most timid students often arrive with one or more friends, and may only say, "I'm just here because you said we had to come." But having them in her office creates an opportunity for her to talk about a recent class topic with the student in a way that initiates a real dialogue, however short, and breaks through the norm in the students' minds that they are "not smart enough" or "not supposed" to ask a professor questions. Making that personal connection with a professor not only helps create the courage to ask questions. It is also vital for building the confidence and finding the mentors or allies required to persevere through the difficult times that everyone will experience at some time while completing a college degree.

Another approach to this phenomenon of students fearing to ask questions has been to identify the misconceptions that students have about what a college class is supposed to entail and how it is supposed to be conducted. An excellent practical exploration of this misconception was done by Rebecca Cox, then professor at New Jersey's Seton Hall University, and detailed in her book *The College Fear Factor.*[6] Through relating her experience of observing college freshman writing classes in session, she gives examples of how a student's fear of speaking out in class or asking questions may be based on false assumptions about appropriate and expected behavior for students and/or for professors. New Majority students have not had the advantage of hearing stories from parents or older siblings about college course experiences. Their first reference point is high school. The many ways in which a university is structured differently in terms of course schedules, study requirements, student supervision, classroom pedagogy, professors' expectations of students, and so forth, are a mystery to New Majority students as they arrive on campus. This problem is aggravated by common myths about college classes that these students often have heard. For instance, the image of college professors which they have acquired from movies and media is usually the lecturer who is the brilliant repository of all knowledge in his field and whose job it is to hand down that knowledge to respectful, note-taking students. Any activity that takes away from this scenario—such as the "Think/Pair/Share" exercise, or similar small-group discussion time, or taking time for multiple questions and even dialogue with students—may be seen by these students as the professor "not doing his job."[7] Obviously, this incorrect preconception of what the college classroom and its professor should be just makes it that much harder for a student to become an active questioner and oral participant in a class. This is why we suggest that early in the course the professor of New Majority students use one or both of the first two suggested strategies, namely, clarifying the role of the professor and/or talking about the importance of being able to ask questions. In this way, a candid discussion of the expectations around and value of asking good questions can be introduced to students' thinking from the beginning.

SUMMARY

Getting students involved in asking thoughtful questions is a vital aspect of activating real student engagement. When professors experiment with one or more of the above strategies, they will find that students gradually learn how to adopt this essential part of an academic identity. Continuing to learn about the familial, social, and cultural attitudes students have toward asking questions will stimulate professors' creativity in finding new, effective approaches.[8]

CHAPTER 6

Engaging Students with Analogies

TWO STUDENTS WERE TALKING to each other over lunch in the cafeteria. Bob sounded pretty upset. "I don't know if I should have signed up for a science class this term. I thought Human Biology would be a course I could do okay in. But it's just so hard!"

George seemed a bit calmer than Bob. He took a big bite out of his hamburger. "What professor do you have for that class, Bob?"

"Professor Anderson. He's always friendly when we come to class, but then he starts teaching and it's just so complicated. There are all these little pieces of information that you have to keep straight about each of the things he tells us about, and it just seems like it's too much to learn. Aren't you taking a science class this term too, George? How do you do it?"

"Yeah. It's Introduction to Chemistry. It's hard too, but I think I'm gradually getting it."

Bob continued looking stressed and commented, "I got the courage last week to ask Professor Anderson if there isn't any way to make this stuff easier to learn. He just said, 'You have to put in the time it takes. There are lots of biological names and descriptions you have to know to pass this class and you just have to learn them.' That wasn't much help for me. Yeah, what *he said was what I already thought. I feel overwhelmed with all those new names and definitions I'm supposed to know!"*

George was thinking about his chemistry class and all the individual elements he was working to learn. Then an image immediately came to mind. "You know, our professor really helped us get a positive attitude about all the details we have to learn. He called it using an 'analogy.' He told us to think of ourselves as running a marathon, not a 500-yard sprint."

Bob countered, "What does running a marathon have to do with chemistry?" "We asked him the same thing," George continued. "Then he started getting us to think about what it would really be like to run a marathon. I have a cousin, Ruben, who does a lot of running, and he actually entered a marathon over in Seattle. So when our professor asked what a marathon run would be like, I shared some of what Ruben told us. He said that the first part felt really good, and he was ahead of a lot of folks. But after not too long, he started to feel like he was running out of breath really bad, so he knew he had to slow down. Ruben said then he felt like just dropping out, because he had let other runners pass him by. He remembered what a coach had told him some time ago: 'Don't look at other runners. Don't compare yourself to them. Concentrate on your own performance.' So he did, and that made him decide he would just keep doing the best he could.

"The route they had to run had some hills. When he was on the side going down, he could go faster and began to feel better about sticking with the whole race. He also told us how there were some stations along the way that had bottles of water available and you could run close to one of those and they would quickly hand you a bottle. When he drank some of it, he got more energy. I guess the whole marathon route was kinda like that—some assists you don't expect and lots of challenges. You just had to take the next part of the race as it came and pace yourself so you could keep going. After a couple of hours, he said he could see the end of the route way ahead, and that was exciting but he was really, really exhausted and his leg was hurting him the last bit of the race. But he actually finished it."

"You talked about all that in your chemistry class?" Bob was puzzled. "How did that help you with all the chemistry stuff you have to learn?"

George's voice was more animated now. "You know, our professor pointed out that learning everything we have to get in chemistry is a lot like running a marathon. We started to see how that was really true. Yeah, we had started off the class being excited and energized by some of the amazing things about matter and chemistry that the professor showed us in the lab. We thought this was going to be a really fun learning experience. Then we started getting into all the stuff we have to memorize and facts we have to know about each element and the combination of elements. It started getting pretty overwhelming. But it really helped when the professor had us think about a marathon and all the steps the runners have to go through to make it to the end. So now when we sound exasperated in class, he reminds us about some part of the marathon, or he asks us what part of the marathon we think we're on right now. It really helps keep me going."

Bob stopped eating for a minute. "I never thought about it that way. That's an awesome idea. I guess I'm going up a hill in my marathon, but I can't stop now!"

WHAT'S GOING ON HERE?

If I were a professor sitting at a table near George and Bob, overhearing their conversation would set me thinking about what seemed natural to me when I was teaching college history classes. Yes, there *are* a lot of individual facts and names and dates to remember in any given history class. You have to expect that; it's part of what history is. Teaching science is very similar; there are lots of individual pieces of information that must be mastered. You can't deal with the big ideas and the major concepts that are most interesting unless you've learned a lot of the basic facts.

Even as a college student, I think I was aware of this necessary challenge in many subject areas and classes. The conversation between George and Bob that I overheard made me suspect that they had not entered their basic chemistry or biology classes with the same expectations that I had. And that set me to thinking about why I wasn't surprised when one of my college classes in a new subject required a whole lot of initial memorizing and organizing basic facts.

What came to mind were the stories my mother told us about her experience at the University of Oregon between 1926 and 1931. She wanted to join the newly developing profession of physical therapy at the first site to offer this post-baccalaureate program, Walter Reed

Hospital in Washington, DC. It required a bachelor's degree in physical education along with science classes taken with the pre-med students. I remember many times when she talked about how demanding the science classes were and how many new facts she had to master. She would demonstrate that when I had hurt myself playing outside; as she was patching me up, she would name every muscle and bone involved. I definitely got the idea that there were a superabundance of new words and facts you learned in college! As I remembered those occasions, I began to realize why I already knew, before I entered my first college class, that there were a lot of challenging, lengthy sets of data to learn in college, especially in science classes. This awareness, I see in retrospect, was one important aspect of the advantages I had as the daughter of college-going parents when I enrolled in college. Being a continuing-generation student gave me a lot of unrecognized advantages.

Listening to George and Bob, I was pretty sure that both of them were first-generation students. But why was George sounding like he could cope with the extensive, demanding content of his science course better than Bob? Was the introduction of an analogy by George's professor, namely a marathon race, what made the difference? Actually, that could be the case, as there are various research studies that have documented the positive effects on learners of using analogies. For instance, Patricia Ann deWinstanley, professor of psychology at Oberlin College in Ohio, points out that using a well-chosen analogy can stimulate a broader range of connections within the learner's mind, making the subject matter more engaging and thus more motivating. When some of these associations have positive and attainable memories attached, the framework through which the learner is viewing the new knowledge can change dramatically.[1]

By talking about the class's learning challenges as if they were a marathon, the professor tapped into a mental image that already has meaning for students. Most students will have been familiar with some aspect of track and field sports, either through their own experience or through that of their siblings or classmates. Many will have watched the Summer Olympics or other national track and field events on television, perhaps including a marathon race. Drawing on these experiences, and filling out their mental images with the kind of detailed information about running a marathon that George recounted to Bob, students' level of stress can be mitigated.[2] This was working for George, because it placed his otherwise overwhelming learning tasks in a context that he could mentally envision. He could imagine himself or someone he knew being involved in a marathon (or perhaps a 10K run at his high school), as a desirable activity that would be fun while requiring a major exertion of effort and perseverance.

ANALOGIES THAT ENGAGE AND MOTIVATE

To make an analogy work effectively, a professor needs to spell out the comparisons that will activate useful mental images. Professor Nina Barcenas, chair of the Science Department at Heritage University, uses the marathon analogy to make the connection between what makes a marathon runner as well as a college student successful. The athlete concentrates only on the specific part of the race he or she is experiencing. Each of them runs at their own pace; no two cross exactly the same spots in the road. The important thing is that every one of them continues running. Parts of the race are smooth and downhill, but parts are hard and uphill. Some parts are harder for some contestants than others. She points out to her students that if you get only 60 percent or 70 percent on a quiz, it's not a failure; you have come that far and you have learned that much already. You can continue working hard to master the next part of the materials and you will do better on the next quiz or test. But it takes constant commitment no matter what a particular part of the class is like for the student, just as the runner must keep going through both easy and hard parts of the route. The challenges of this particular class are very similar to a marathon contest, and Professor Barcenas's students can picture themselves along the marathon route and can look with new eyes on their need to continue pushing themselves to master the next part of the course.

Professor Barcenas uses another analogy successfully to urge overwhelmed students to keep learning the myriad scientific facts she presents in her biology classes. She tells them that each new fact they are learning is like a single piece of a large jigsaw puzzle. By itself, each jigsaw piece has little meaning. But as you pick up more pieces and begin to fit them together, parts of the puzzle become recognizable—an ear and a tail become a dog, a tower and a window become a castle. As each smaller section begins to make sense, you start to see how these parts are going together to make a whole. Finally, five hundred or a thousand pieces later, an entire picture emerges, and you recognize how everything contributes to a completed picture. She points out to her class, "That's why you can't get discouraged while you are learning the pieces I am teaching you this week!"

Selecting Analogies

The marathon and jigsaw puzzle analogies are examples that can be used to help motivate students when the course material seems overwhelming. They are what we might call "general analogies" because they apply to the entire process of learning in a course or perhaps even in an entire degree program. The most important aspect of choosing and using a general analogy to encourage students is ensuring that the analogy speaks directly to their experience. So what you choose will depend upon the specific characteristics of your students. It is wise to conduct some informal testing of the subject of analogies you plan to use, to be sure that students are familiar with the mental images that you plan to call on in your analogy. This can be done indirectly and informally in chats with students before or after class, or when you see them on campus. To use an example related to the jigsaw analogy, you could mention a jigsaw puzzle being done at your home or that of a relative either now or in the past, as a way to talk about informal, relaxing activities in your life and theirs. From their reactions you can surmise whether or not they, too, have done jigsaw puzzles. If they appear to be familiar with this activity, then you can feel confident when you use the jigsaw analogy in a more serious classroom setting that their mental images related to that activity will help you to communicate with them.

Recently I had an opportunity to see an inadvertent example of what happens when someone does not choose an analogy that relates to the audience's experiences. At an interfaith Thanksgiving service, attended primarily by low-income local residents, many of whom are farm laborers, the speaker was trying to make the point that it is a long and winding pathway in our lives for us to develop all the qualities and strengths that we wish. He started by talking about how extensive and complicated it looks when you begin to play eighteen holes of golf. It is a very long walk from each hole to the next one, and you have to do this eighteen times. You have so many clubs to choose from as you plan your next stroke. You have to use an entirely different approach to the ball and the next stroke if you are on the putting green, as contrasted with how you proceed if you are making a long shot as you begin a new hole that is many yards down the green from where you are standing. Then there are sand traps and perhaps some water hazards too, and you probably have to navigate out of at least one of those during your round of golf, not to mention the frustration of losing one or more balls.

I glanced around the room, and everyone was looking politely at the preacher or staring at the floor. No heads nodded as he talked about the various scenarios in the golf game, and no one chuckled when he referred to the sand traps, water hazards, or lost balls. Perhaps he sensed the problem, because he soon switched his analogy to talking about what it takes to prepare a major Thanksgiving feast for you and your relatives. He talked about ordering the turkey ahead of time, cleaning the house, setting the table, getting out special dishes, cooking some things in the days before, making desserts, and getting ready for everyone sitting around the TV afterwards. Almost immediately the reactions of those in the room changed. Heads nodded, murmurs of agreement or disagreement floated in the air, and smiles or laughs greeted some of the speaker's more humorous descriptions. The audience had all experienced what he was speaking about, and it was easy for them to apply this analogy to the bigger challenge of focusing one's life on the values and virtues that make living worthwhile, in spite of all the various interruptions and detours that impinge on our lives.

For general analogies to be effective, they must relate in very real terms to the audience—in this case, to our students. A premise of this book is that most of us in the professoriate come from backgrounds with significant differences from those of our New Majority students. Dr. Lori Arviso Alvord, MD, the first Navajo woman surgeon, brings these differences to life when she talks about her experience of entering Dartmouth College. Although what she mentions is specific to the Navajo culture, it reminds us that many of our New Majority students come from nondominant cultures, each having its own unique view of the world and what constitutes appropriate behavior. Dr. Alvord's litany of differences reminds us of the various categories we should consider in watching for communication mismatches and looking for analogies that will help.

> Although I felt lucky to be there [at Dartmouth], I was in complete culture shock. I thought people talked too much, laughed too loud, asked too many personal questions, and had no respect for privacy. They seemed overly competitive and put a higher value on material wealth than I was used to . . . [As Navajos] we were taught to be humble and not to draw attention to ourselves, to favor cooperation over competition (so as not to make ourselves "look better" at another's expense or hurt someone's feelings), to value silence over words, to respect our elders, and to reserve our opinions until they were asked for.[3]

Knowing how extensive and complex the sociocultural differences may be for New Majority students makes it a bit more challenging to choose analogies that will work. As mentioned earlier, if you have doubts about whether a general analogy would speak to your students, you can try it out informally with one or two students and watch their reactions. You will be able to tell immediately if they are relating to the mental picture you are trying to create for them.

This is particularly important to try in advance if your analogy comes from family home life and how children are raised. Differences in these areas of life are notoriously common among various different cultures or socioeconomic classes, as the above example from a young Navajo woman demonstrates, but frequently those in the mainstream culture are unaware of these dissimilarities because they have never had the opportunity to observe them in the homes of people from those cultures. A simple example of home differences I heard about from local friends several years ago was this. First-graders were given a test that was intended to demonstrate their cognitive development; it involved sets of pictures. Kids were told that for each set of pictures, they should mark the two pictures that "go together." One picture set consisted of a cup, a saucer, a spoon, and a chair. Virtually all the children marked the cup and the spoon as belonging together, and this was counted as an incorrect answer in the scoring guide. Their teachers told me that in all the local homes they knew (their own and others), no one used saucers with cups. You set the cup right on the table. But you needed a spoon to stir in the sugar or cream in coffee, so kids picked the spoon to go with the cup. Obviously, this particular test was not a good measure of cognitive ability for those children! Applying this incident to the task of choosing an appropriate analogy, if a professor were trying to use the analogy of putting a cup on a saucer at the dining room table, it would have no meaning to those young people who grew up in homes where cups did not come with saucers. Trying out a potential analogy that depends upon family or home practices with one or two students will let you know if you can feel confident in explicating that specific analogy with your whole class.

Focused Analogies for Specific Concepts

There is another way in which analogies can be useful in facilitating student learning. While general analogies are useful for overall motivation, since they apply to a major component of the student's challenges or the overall realities of a subject area, such as earning a degree or mastering a myriad of facts and principles in a major, *focused analogies* can be helpful in teaching a specific concept. Focused analogies address a more limited concept and have been used especially in teaching science, but they have a place in other disciplines as well. In teaching a history course, I may need to explain what a "primary source" is. One focused analogy I could use would be talk that has been passed on from one extended family member to another. Suppose Cousin A tells me something I'm surprised to hear, namely that Cousin B's family is moving to Phoenix next month, which Cousin A says she heard from her nephew who was told that by his aunt. I may be a bit suspicious of this information's validity, so I call up Cousin B and learn directly from him that he and his family are taking a vacation in Phoenix next month and may also investigate, as they vacation, the possibility of moving there in the future. My conversation with Cousin B is like a "primary source," and the information I received from Cousin A, or her nephew or his aunt, are all "secondary sources." This focused analogy allows me to explore in more detail why primary sources are important in history research and how my students can identify whether a source they find is really a primary source or a secondary source.

Patricia Ann deWinstanley describes a problem familiar to most professors, for which a focused analogy might provide a useful solution:

> If asked, all of us who lecture to students would affirm that our goal is to have students learn from the lectures. If what we mean, however, is that the goal is to have students actually learn during lectures, as opposed to their learning (or not learning) from later activities, such as going over their notes from the lecture, we face no small challenge. By the very definition of learning, achieving such a goal requires that lectures trigger in students the types of processes that result in durable encoding of the concepts, facts, and ideas covered in the lecture.[4]

If real learning requires "durable encoding" to occur—meaning that a new idea becomes embedded in more permanent ways in the brain, through such means as vivid images or connections to already-gained knowledge—then it is imperative that a vehicle to facilitate the encoding be available to the learners. As Dr. deWinstanley puts it, "Learning does not happen, for example, through some kind of literal recording process. Rather, learning is an interpretive process: new information is stored by relating it to, or linking it up with, what is already known."[5] A focused analogy that utilizes something the student already knows can be the vehicle that makes effective learning possible.

Focused analogies, as well as general analogies, are often used in speeches as a way to keep the attention of the audience on the topic and speaker by creating vivid images in the mind of listeners. It's a practice also very helpful to professors as they give lectures or presentations to their classes. Someone who was famous for using both kinds of analogies with great effect was Martin Luther King Jr. Here are some examples that may inspire you to find creative analogies for the difficult topics you teach.

- "Darkness cannot drive out darkness: only light can do that. Hate cannot drive out hate: only love can do that."[6] (Note that the first sentence creates a visual image in the mind of the listeners so that they have an image to which they can attach the abstract concepts of hate and love.)
- "I refuse to accept the idea that man is mere flotsam and jetsam in the river of life, unable to influence the unfolding events which surround him."[7]
- "Every time I take a flight, I am always mindful of the many people who make a successful journey possible—the known pilots and the unknown ground crew. You honor the dedicated pilots of our struggle who have sat at the controls as the freedom movement soared into orbit . . . You honor the ground crew without whose labor and sacrifices the jet flights to freedom could never have left the earth."[8]

Matrix Method of Developing Analogies

Creating appropriate focused analogies as you introduce new topics helps students become more fully engaged in this new learning. Here's a simple way to uncover an appropriate focused analogy that you can use for a new concept or area of study, based on the approach developed by Janis Bulgren, a research professor at the University of Kansas Center for Research, and her colleagues.[9]

1. Make a table or matrix with three columns and an overall heading identifying the concept or topic for which you are creating an analogy.
2. Label the columns like this:
   a. Column A: *Topic's Essential Traits*
   b. Column B: *Analogy's Similar Traits*
   c. Column C: *Dissimilar Traits*
3. In column A, *Topic's Essential Traits*, list the key characteristics of the topic you want to teach.
4. Study the items you have entered in column A and brainstorm about possible analogies that would have similar key characteristics. Choose one of the analogies that comes to mind.

5. Using the analogy you picked, for each of the characteristics you entered in a row under column A, enter a matching characteristic from your analogy in column B or leave it blank if no similar characteristic exists.
6. Now fill out column C by noting any characteristic that is true of your topic (column A), but not true of your analogy (column B is blank) and put an X in column C in that row.
7. If there are several X's in your matrix, you may wish to choose a different analogy and fill out another matrix to see if another analogy is a better match with your topic.

By utilizing the matrix approach to choose an analogy, you can identify the key elements of the analogy that may make the idea you are teaching clearer to students. You can also be prepared to comment on aspects of the analogy that are neither similar nor useful for understanding the main concept.

Analogies as "Attention Enhancers"

In the course of conducting research on the use of analogies in teaching, I have noted that several authors make a point of cautioning that while analogies are useful for engaging students, especially when the topic seems very obscure or complex to the learners, there are definite limitations.

If the topic to be taught is already a familiar area of knowledge to learners, analogies are not necessary to facilitate acquiring the new knowledge of the topic. In fact, use of an analogy that takes the learners away from thinking in an area that is already familiar to them may actually slow down their learning. On the other hand, if the subject is quite unfamiliar to the students, the use of an appropriate analogy will speed up and deepen students' knowledge acquisition.[10]

Like every other helpful strategy to engage students more fully in their learning, analogies have their place but are not a panacea and are not always appropriate or useful. When professors pick insightful analogies with many parallels to the key elements of concepts being taught, students' brains are stimulated with clear and tangible images. Having a lively image to focus on creates what Greta Freeman and Pamela Wash at the University of South Carolina Upstate call "attention enhancers": "The use of attention enhancers based on brain-compatible learning research serves three purposes: to gain students' attention quickly, to sustain students' attention throughout the range of each class meeting, and to ensure students will remember much of the information provided in each class meeting."[11]

Another approach utilizing analogies is highlighted by Ken Bain, director of the Center for Teaching Excellence at New York University. In his research interviewing the most effective professors, he noted this interesting observation: "The people we explored know the value that intellectual challenges—even inducing puzzlement and confusion—can play in stimulating interest in the questions of their courses. Several of them talked about finding the novel, the incongruous, and the paradoxical. With carefully chosen analogies they make even the familiar seem strange and intriguing and the strange appear familiar."[12]

Summary

Exploring the broad possibilities that analogies have to engage students, we have reviewed both their amazing potential and the possible pitfalls that a poorly chosen analogy can produce. Technical and science fields are generally easier areas in which to identify insight-producing analogies, but virtually any field can be enlivened with just the right comparison, provided that the analogy's components are carefully examined with students. Analogies, properly used, and geared to the specific students who need help to become engaged in the learning process, can be outstanding examples of "attention enhancers."

PART TWO

STRATEGIES TO PROMOTE A SENSE OF BELONGING

IT IS PROBABLY a fair generalization to say that almost all new college students, both first-generation and continuing-generation, start out with initial questions about whether they will like their college, whether they will do well in classes, and whether or not they will persevere to a degree. Those who come from families where parents or older siblings have earned degrees normally come with expectations that at least some aspects of college will be enjoyable and that, even if difficult, the experience will be worthwhile in the long run. While the "homesick period" is often a challenge for both continuing-generation and first-generation resident students during the first semester or quarter, most of the continuing-generation students overcome this feeling by late in the first term and begin to feel that they really do belong at their college. In the terminology of communication mismatch theory, these continuing-generation students experience mostly "communication matches" with their professors and campus administrative staff and fellow students. This is frequently not the case for first-generation students. In the next section we will explore three strategies that can lead to first-generation students moving from feelings of discomfort or alienation or intimidation to feeling a sense of belonging at college. The strategies start with ideas for using the first days of class to help students feel comfortable with fellow students, with the professor, and with the course's syllabus. Faculty can also engender feelings of belonging from New Majority students by making efforts to understand logistical and related barriers students experience in finding the time and places to study. The third strategy shared in this section describes ways to tap into the community values that many New Majority students share in order to develop their feelings of belonging and encourage their perseverance to graduation.

CHAPTER 7

Welcoming Students with First-Day Activities

ALEXA AND TRINA walked out of the class together on the first day of the term and started across the college campus.

"Hey, I'm so happy that you are in this class, Trina!" Alexa looked down and gave a long sigh as they started walking across campus. "I just keep asking myself if I really belong here, 'cuz things are so confusing." After another long pause she added, "But when I saw you, I started feeling a little better."

They had been friends in high school, and Alexa was happy to find herself in the same class with Trina as she began her first term at the university. Alexa pulled a stapled set of papers out of her armload of books and waved it in front of Trina.

"This was something that made me feel really like maybe this college stuff isn't for me," Alexa said. "Why did Professor Moore give us this big set of papers? She used some name for it I didn't know. Sounded like 'sill-a-buy'?"

"Yeah," Trina replied. "One of the other students sitting near me spelled it for me: it's called a 'syll-a-bus'—S-Y-L-L-A-B-U-S. See, here's the word at the top of the first page. That's a new word to me! Professor Moore didn't say if we were supposed to do anything with it when she passed it out. Seemed like she thought we knew what it was."

Alexa giggled a little and said, "Hmm. Syllabus. I call it a 'silly-buy'—something I'd never spend money to buy, 'cuz I don't know what to do with it!"

Trina grinned at Alexa's pun. "A 'silly-buy'? That's a good way to remember the word, anyway. I kinda remember that they mentioned it in our New Student Orientation, but I don't remember what we were supposed to do with it. I know it won't do any good to ask my mom when I get home. Being as I'm the first one to try college, and my mom is always saying, 'You sure you want to keep going to school instead of taking that job they offered you at the restaurant?' These things keep happening that make me feel so much like an outsider, so I don't know."

Alexa responded, "I suppose we could ask Professor Moore after class tomorrow. But she seems kinda formal. I know I've always been told to be respectful and just listen, and then I'll figure it out, but I'm not so sure if that's true here. It was pretty hard keeping up taking notes today, and I feel kinda lost, too."

Trina reached over and took the syllabus out of Alexa's hand. "Look at this. The first page has a bunch of stuff we already know, like the name of the class, what time it meets, that we have to arrive on time, what day the final exam is at the end of the term." Trina rifled through the stack of pages and added, "The rest of it looks sort of like an outline for the professor so she knows what she's gonna do every day in our class. I don't see why we need it."

Alexa agreed. "Don't know why Professor Moore's giving it to us. Looks like it's really for her." Trina handed the syllabus back to Alexa, who stuck the syllabus inside the cover of one of the books she was carrying.

WHAT'S GOING ON HERE?

It's obvious that Trina and Alexa are experiencing some of the "I wonder if I really belong here" syndrome that so many New Majority students feel. This short episode helps us realize that knowing others in the class alleviates some of the anxiety. Alexa seeing Trina in the class helped her feel a little bit more relaxed. At the same time, not having the courage to ask questions and not being given explanations for something new to students but taken for granted by the professor—the syllabus—are two factors that can exacerbate the students' feeling of not belonging, and it's especially important to set a tone of belonging during that initial class meeting.

In this chapter we are considering how class experiences on the first day of the term can be used to lessen the feelings of not belonging for New Majority students. We'll start by looking at a typical first-day activity—distributing a syllabus for the course.

Most high school teachers do not employ a syllabus, so it's easy to see why New Majority students, when they arrive at their first-term classes, wouldn't be familiar with its purpose. But it is not only the brand-new students in a class who may need help to see the syllabus as a welcome and welcoming tool from the professor. Professors might presume that during students' earlier classes, their professors would have introduced them to a syllabus and how it should be used, especially if the institution requires professors to present a syllabus in each class. However, the reality is that some professors may have passed out a syllabus but not given any explanation. New students may have been too nervous or intimidated to ask, "What's this for?" especially if the continuing-generation students (non–New Majority students) in the class looked like they knew what it was and didn't pose any questions. Another factor may be that some New Majority students may have missed the first day or two of classes in a previous term and therefore missed receiving the syllabus with the explanations that were given. All of these reasons, as well as other scenarios you can imagine, create an unexpected situation for many professors who presume that students know why they are receiving a syllabus. To avoid these unintended mismatches between professors' expectations and students' experience, professors who teach New Majority students need to involve them in actively reading and understanding the syllabus at the outset of each class. When students see the syllabus as a resource that is important to their success, professors will be rewarded with knowing that their syllabi are indeed worth the time they invested in developing them. Later in this chapter you'll find some creative ways to get students to use your syllabus.

But before we turn to those strategies, let's look at another reality that is intertwined with the syllabus issue. As we listen to Trina and Alexa talking about their first day in Professor Moore's class, we hear them both express unwillingness to ask her about the syllabus. There may be various reasons for their hesitancy. It might be their anxiety level about being able to fit into college. It could be related to the professor's reaction to a student's question during the class. It could also flow from their subliminal cultural norms regarding asking questions. Let's consider in detail these last two reasons that might be keeping Trina and Alexa from asking the questions about the syllabus that they should be asking.

The first reason refers to students who are not always afraid to ask questions; they are often willing to pose intelligent queries when the subject matter is not clear. But they are highly sensitive to how the professor responds to questions asked during class. When the professor appears to welcome questions and to honor the intelligent thinking that led to the question, those students will freely ask questions. But if the professor appears, even subtly, to be at all frustrated by a question, those students will not risk posing a query.

How might this first deterrent to questioning have occurred for Trina and Alexa? In launching the first day's class, Professor Moore may have made the point that she expects students to know the "basics" that underlie the new material of this class, as part of her strategy to set high standards, which is certainly a laudable goal. She may have also made this point because of feeling a certain amount of pressure, faced with teaching a course that has a significant amount of content and only one term to cover it all. With that gnawing concern in the background, Professor Moore may be unaware that when she responded to a student's question about the syllabus, she sounded, or looked, just a little exasperated when asked something she presumed was already in the knowledge base of the students.

For continuing-generation students, unless they are particularly shy, this behavior by the professor will probably not deter them from asking additional questions in the future. But from the viewpoint of first-generation students, they may be already doubting whether they should be in this environment ("I'm not sure if I belong in college!") So if a professor's reaction to another student's question—perhaps a slight eye movement or pursed lips or raised tone of voice—implies "I thought you should already know that," the first-generation students' reticence will be greatly heightened. This reaction can be viewed as an example of stereotype threat being experienced by the New Majority student. When she feels stressed in the presence of the professor, because she is feeling the professor might not believe she belongs in the class, she is hypersensitive to any indication of a negative reaction on the professor's part.[1]

This means that Professor Moore has a special challenge on the first day of class to appear relaxed and accepting of students, no matter what questions or concerns they express. Such factors as tone of voice, speaking more loudly or slower or faster than usual, raising an eyebrow, avoiding direct eye contact with the student, interrupting the student, and other nonverbal subtle communication clues will convey to sensitive students—especially the New Majority ones—that the professor is not entirely at ease with or accepting of them. This mismatch between the actual thoughts of the professor, who is feeling only the time pressure of the course, and the interpretation by a New Majority student, can be a conclusion that appears logical to a New Majority student, given her prior self-questioning. She can be thinking, "I had the same question as that other student just asked! The professor obviously thought we should already know that, and she's probably right. I really doubt if I belong in this class." If this happens during the first session or two of the course, a New Majority student may drop the class while the withdrawal period allows her to do so. If asked for a reason, she will probably say she really wasn't prepared for that class. She presumes that the professor's behavior is normal and that the problem is her own unpreparedness to be a student in that class. On the other hand, if the student does remain in the class, it will be exceedingly hard for her to ask the professor a question in future sessions.

Many experienced professors, having taught mostly continuing-generation students, have said that occasionally expressing their frustration at what students don't know generally does not slow down the future questioning behavior of most of them. They've seen professors frustrated with students' lack of knowledge before and observed that this is only a temporary glitch in most student-professor communication. However, when these professors learn about New Majority students' feeling a lack of belonging, it motivates them to carefully adapt their behavior in the early sessions of a course to avoid triggering students' permanent "clamming up" or even course withdrawal. I am not underestimating the adaptations some professors need to make to their communication styles, because these are often subtle, unintended communication behaviors that have not been a concern with continuing-gen students before. Yet they can have a significant negative effect on the success goals the professor has for New Majority students.

The second reason that New Majority students might not be asking about the syllabus, or other new and mysterious aspects of the class, may relate to their sociocultural backgrounds. As discussed earlier, there are many sociocultural groups who discourage question-asking. Professor Gutierrez Spencer, working at an institution with a large number of minority students, offers this advice: "Understand that many minority students' form of showing 'respect' is so extreme, it seems like passivity. They are also very respectful towards each other. This precludes any one 'showing off' or 'standing out from the crowd.'"[2] These New Majority students may not be as tempted to drop the class entirely, but they have definitely been conditioned by their cultural upbringing regarding questioning behavior to respond very differently than academic culture expects. Their ability to learn as readily and in as much depth as their professors desire may be handicapped if they cannot adapt to the academic cultural norm of asking questions whenever needed or appropriate. In a previous chapter we explored this challenge in more depth, and we don't need to repeat that here. But the issue of asking questions also interrelates with the matter of establishing a sense of belonging on the first day as well as making the syllabus a useful resource for students. To be effective with New Majority students, Professor Moore would need to plan a review of the syllabus that involves students directly, even though they have not asked any questions about it, making sure that the syllabus is a useful instrument for them.

STARTING OFF RIGHT

In this section I will share several strategies that can help students feel a bit more like they belong in college and in your class, while at the same time showing them how to use the course syllabus and helping them move into the academic culture.

Create Smaller Groups from the Outset

It may seem obvious, but the mere fact of putting students into small groups where they are with a few of their fellow students, and making clear that this grouping will continue to be a basic unit throughout the term, creates a bridge for New Majority students to begin identifying with other students and thinking of themselves as belonging in the course and the college.

If the classroom has movable tables and/or chairs, the professor can rearrange this furniture into smaller groupings where students will be facing each other. Groupings of no fewer than four students and no larger than ten students will work. Having these settings in place as a student enters the room means that each must choose one of the groups and take a seat there. As more students enter, each will be inclined to sit in a group where at least some of those already there appear to be friendly or compatible.

Not every classroom has chairs or tables that can be rearranged into groups. In this case, the professor can use various methods to assign students in groups, as described in the next paragraph. After assigning each student to a specific group, you can ask students to change seats so that they are sitting in the vicinity of the other members of their group, allowing them to talk with each other when asked to do so. Naming the group membership yourself is preferable to letting students choose their own group. If the professor lets students form their own units it is likely that those who already know each other will gravitate to the same group. This deprives those students of learning, both social and academic, that can result from being in a group with individuals who are new to each other.

There are many random ways to set up groups. Professors may want to use their own or develop their own twist on one of the following:

- Use an alphabetical list of all students in the class and choose every sixth or eighth or tenth name on the list to be in the first group, every fifth, seventh or ninth to be in the second group, and so forth.
- If students are sitting in rows, identify each sixth or eighth or tenth chair to be members of the first group. Repeat the process with the next chairs until all have been assigned. This method deliberately

breaks up any cluster that has formed from students who know each other sitting next to their buddies. You can also have students count off, one to six or eight or ten, and then have all with the same number move into one grouping, sitting near one another.

- Ask students to raise their hand when you name an already-existing identifier that they belong to, within a category. Form student units that mix up the various subcategories. For instance, name six, eight, or ten neighborhoods or cities that students come from and form a group with members from each of those places of residence; or list several sports or sports teams and ask which is each one's favorite; or name the possible number of siblings from zero to seven; or with a larger class, have the students identify the month when each one's birthday occurs; or use other nonjudgmental categories that have at least six mutually exclusive items within the category.

Help Students Make Connections with Each Other

On the first day of class, take a few minutes to help students begin to get acquainted with their small group and with the professor. One highly structured but very useful approach has been identified by students of Professor Dan Peters at Yakima Valley Community College as helping them feel a real part of the class right from the first day. Professor Peters asks them immediately in the first class session to write down:

- two questions they would like to ask the student on their right;
- two assumptions they are making about the student on their left;
- two assumptions about this class; and finally
- two questions they would like to ask him.

He clarifies how to develop their questions by telling them not to ask things that are too general, like what year the student is in college, but also not to ask something too personal. He gives them examples: "Ask them something like what their favorite class was in high school and why, or how far they've ever been away from home and where they went." After students have written down their questions, he allows a short amount of time for students to share their questions with the classmate on their right and hear their answers, and then time to share their assumptions with the classmate on their left and hear the responses.

This first process starts building trust and relationships among the students and forms a first step to a sense of belonging in the class.

Then Professor Peters tells them that part of their homework for the next class session is to read the syllabus carefully and after reading it to write two questions about the class that were not answered in the document. He cautions them to read carefully, so they won't write a question that is actually already answered in the syllabus. That would show that they hadn't really read it.

Next he turns to their assumptions about the class, which he asks them to read aloud. One of the key reasons for asking about their assumptions is to address misconceptions they have about the class, which often form barriers to their success. For New Majority students, getting these assumptions out of the way may be crucial for their perseverance and success, because these assumptions may be beliefs that are subtly programming them for failure even before they start. For instance, if they assume that "quite a few students usually flunk this class" or similar negative thoughts, the students' stress level will be heightened to a point that it will inhibit their success. If they assume there is a requirement that is probably beyond their ability, like having to write a fifty-page paper, this expectation can program them for discouragement and dropping the class. Professor Peters addresses these kinds of assumptions firmly, undermining the barriers that New Majority students may have brought with them to class. If a student mentions an assumption that is clearly explained differently or refuted in the syllabus, he doesn't comment on it except to tell the student, "Check out that assumption as you do the homework I just gave you to read the syllabus. Ask again tomorrow if you don't find the information related to your assumption."

Then he moves to the questions about himself. At this point, students will often look at each other and smile in anticipation of some of the questions that might be posed to the professor. That is exactly why Professor Peters uses this strategy. By dedicating a small portion of the first day's class to their questions about him, he is helping students overcome any feeling of intimidation they may feel toward him and building a sense of being connected with him and with the class. It also will overcome any inadvertent reaction he had to a student's comment or question earlier in the class, which might have intimidated students struggling with their first-gen stereotype threat. He tells the class that he will answer their questions candidly, unless they are too personal and then he may take a "pass."

When I interviewed Professor Peters and observed his class, I noted that usually students ask him things such as whether he has any kids, how old they are, where he got his college education and advanced degrees, and similar objective facts. Usually some students are a little braver and ask things like what makes him lose his temper, or what he wants for Christmas, or what's the hardest thing he has ever done. By responding to their questions as candidly as he can and using the "pass" only when necessary, and by including some humor whenever possible, the class begins to visibly relax. Smiles appear on many faces as he speaks, and students exchange amused glances with each other. A feeling is building across the room that "we're all in this together," which is exactly what Professor Peters is after. Making all students feel they belong is now a real possibility.

Use the Syllabus to Help Students Feel in Charge of Their Learning

Many New Majority students, especially as they enter higher education for the first time, have only the vaguest sense of what college is really like. Most of their high school experiences were entirely teacher-driven. Success depended upon following carefully the specific steps that teachers dictated and frequently reviewed.

As college students realize that they are more "on their own now," those who have college-educated parents or relatives often ask them many questions about how college works. New Majority students do not have that option. Well-written and carefully explained syllabi can fill some of that gap for them.

Professors who teach many first-gen students have frequently developed simple but clever ways to help students understand how the syllabus can be a guiding light for them in a class. Several professors at Heritage University give a quiz on the second day of class, following the first day's assignment to read the syllabus carefully. They ask questions that can be answered by information found in the syllabus, and some even allow the students to consult the syllabus as they write the answers to five or ten quiz items. The items are chosen to reinforce key aspects of the class that students need to keep in the forefront of their minds. For instance, the quiz may ask the due dates for in-class presentations, or deadlines for completing important reading assignments. And students get five points for correctly completing the quiz, even if they have to consult the syllabus again to get the answers. This additional motivation introduces the students to the point system of grading in the class, and gives them the positive reinforcement of earning some points at the very outset of the class.

Dr. Laura Gutierrez Spencer at New Mexico State University, Las Cruces, has found that she can successfully explain the importance of her syllabus to Chicano Studies students by pointing out that it is a contract between the students and the professor. She makes this suggestion to teachers: "Explain that you as the faculty member are also expected to adhere to the basics of the syllabus (evaluation standards, the number of exams and papers, etc.). Explain how this contract also protects students' rights."[3]

Another approach used by Professor Peters is to give the students a copy of the syllabus that has blank lines where strategic pieces of information should be. He then walks through the syllabus with the students, stopping at each blank to name the content that should be there, and waiting while students fill it in. Such items as the professor's office hours and e-mail address, or instructions for getting on the website where course resources are located, are good pieces of information for students to write themselves so the information is actually passing through their brains.

From many occasions of using this exercise, Professor Peters has learned to watch students carefully as they work through this exercise. He may notice that one or more of the items do not appear to be well understood or meaningful. This gives him an opportunity to clarify any such items. One of those may be "office hours." As a New Majority student who is now a Heritage senior said to me recently, "I didn't have any idea what 'office hours' were. It sounded like something for the professor to do in his office. I had no idea why the syllabus always told us what the 'office hours' were. I think I'd been attending classes for more than a year before another student said something that made me understand: those hours were the ones for us! It changed my whole way of thinking, because then I knew it was okay to go talk to the professor in his office. Before that, I thought I would be interrupting him and it would be very rude and not help my grade at all."

FIRST DAY OF CLASS FOR STUDENTS BEYOND FIRST YEAR

Some first-day activities that address issues of full engagement and belonging are also appropriate and helpful to students who are not in their first year at the university. One area of concern for students from freshman year through junior and even senior year is how they view the textbook required in the course. One of the Heritage University professors, Edwin Rousculp, developed a creative solution when he found that students in his sophomore or junior level courses were sometimes dismissive of the textbook and only expected to pick it up when a specific reading assignment of certain pages was required.[4]

In most cases, there are many additional resources between the covers of the textbook in addition to the straightforward readings of each chapter. These include diagrams, sidebars with supplemental information, charts, bibliographies, footnotes or endnotes with extensive references, and a robust index. Many of these resources can be very helpful to students when they are given any assignment that reaches beyond reading the chapter. For instance, when they are asked to pick an interesting topic from the chapter and bring additional information on it to class, students often don't realize that the best springboard to finding this additional material may well be in the references, bibliography, or index in their own textbook.

To give students a practical experience of engaging their textbook, Professor Rousculp invented an exercise he calls "The Text Hunt." In teams of two, students receive a list of questions that must be answered by finding the information in the textbook. The two-student team approach assures that everyone will have a textbook to work with, since some students in the class may not have bought the book yet or perhaps do not intend to buy it. Depending upon the class and its enrollees, the professor may also run this exercise as a contest among the two-person teams for the fastest completion or the most accurate and/or comprehensive answers.

Here are some examples of questions on a typical Text Hunt guide:

- On page [xx] there is a diagram illustrating an organizational structure. Find two other places in the book where the lowest-level roles in this diagram are mentioned. One place should contain more information on this role.
- Study the table of contents and list the sections that are common to all chapters. Hint: These sections usually come at the beginning and end of each chapter. Tell briefly the purpose of each of these common sections.
- If you wanted to learn more about the research behind [concept X], where would you look in the text for a reference? Copy at least one bibliographic entry when you find it and identify where you found it.
- Locate a graph within one of the chapters. Study the graph and write three inferences or conclusions you can make from this graph.
- Find an entry in the index that lists at least three different places where that topic can be found in the text. Look up each of these places and write a one-sentence summary describing what aspect of this topic is covered in each of these places.
- After you have completed the exercises in this Text Hunt, what questions have arisen in your mind? Write them down, and star the ones that interest you the most.

If you decide to develop a Text Hunt exercise for your class, try to include a least one question in each of these categories:

- Requires reading a footnote or endnote
- Requires interpreting a graph
- Requires using the index to locate several widely separated places in the textbook that deal with the same topic
- Requires finding the name of books and/or article(s) for further research on a specific topic from the text's bibliography or footnotes
- Requires gathering information conveyed through a diagram
- Requires combining two or more of the above activities

When professors use this activity on the first day of class, several positive outcomes usually result.[5] First, students who were not planning to buy the textbook are more likely to do so, and the professor can mention the availability of financial aid to assist in the purchase, if appropriate. Second, students are simultaneously learning of the additional resources found in the textbook and practicing critical thinking and analytical skills. Third, students are experiencing this class as engaged learning; this programs them to expect full engagement in future classes and discourages personal activities during class, such as texting their friends. As they complete this exercise, students begin to have questions that the course will address during the term, and this draws them into the subject from the first day. Fourth, when an assignment requires outside research, students are more apt to consult the valid sources referenced in the textbook rather than depending entirely on the uneven quality of resources accessed through Googling. In a course that will require writing a research paper with references, the Text Hunt can direct students to list the "answer" in the form of a correctly formatted footnote or endnote reference, which will give them practice at this skill. In summary, a well-planned Text Hunt exercise provides a dynamic, engaging, and "high impact" way to launch students in any course on the path to active involvement and success.[6]

Although this book focuses on first-gen students, it should be noted also that continuing-generation students, according to Professor Mark Canada, professor and vice chancellor at Indiana University, Kokomo, also need some carefully calculated approaches to the course syllabus. Otherwise they may see this document as primarily an outline for the benefit of the professor as he charts the way through the class. Canada describes some approaches that will change this incorrect view by helping students see that the syllabus can be a significant help to them. For instance, he suggests that in writing their syllabi, professors use plain language that communicates friendliness. Saying "I welcome you to contact me" rather than "If you need to contact me," and similar small changes in traditional wording, can make the student feel a part of the class from the beginning. Regarding the objectives of the course, a key element in any syllabus, he provides a delightful example of how he has expressed this for a literature course:

Imagine a road trip that could take you all over America, showing you exotic locales, introducing you to interesting characters, and dropping you in the middle of wild adventures. You will set sail on the high seas, stalk through the wilds of Virginia, and stroll down the streets of Philadelphia. You will meet powerful leaders and oppressed slaves, pious Christians and fiendish villains. You will experience passionate love and abject terror. Best of all, you will return home not exhausted and defeated, but refreshed and enlightened.[7]

In the case of both first- and continuing-generation students, professors need to take special care to engage students directly with the syllabus at the outset of the class. In addition to ideas mentioned above, professors can use the small groups that are established on the first day to have students engage with the syllabus. Give each group a different question or task, and after having time to do this assigned work, each group can report back to the whole class. Especially for first-generation students, causing them to interact with the syllabus in one way or another will help them feel more in charge of their learning, which in turn helps establish that crucial atmosphere of belonging. The course syllabus can be not just a requirement from the dean's office, but an effective learning strategy that any professor can utilize for increased student success.

Whatever method the professor chooses, it is important that students have read the syllabus; have entered the due dates for assignments in their own calendars or to-do lists; have understood how to get hold of the professor via phone, office hours, and e-mail; and have seen from the topics listed that a significant amount of study time on one's own will be required to keep up with the flow of content during the course.[8] Making sure that all students have this level of comprehension from the syllabus will go a long way toward making New Majority students feel that they do belong in this course. It will motivate them to take the dedicated time needed and to give the quality of concentration necessary to pass the class.

SUMMARY

This chapter has been devoted to some considerations for making the first class session of each course into a welcoming bridge for New Majority students. By helping them create connections with their fellow students and their professor from the very first day, and by assisting them to clearly visualize through the syllabus what this course will entail and how they can succeed in it, first-generation students can truly feel that they are an active and valued part of this class and their college. The importance of this comes home to me as I recall an incident with a first-generation student who was a research assistant with me several years ago. Louise was the first in her family to finish high school or to enroll in college, and she had several young children and a husband who had no postsecondary education. As she reached senior year status, having earned outstanding grades in her course work, she was chosen to travel to a weekend intercollegiate event and give a presentation at the University of Washington. When she came back home from the event, I asked her how it had gone. She answered with enthusiasm. "My presentation went really well. You know, maybe now I can say to myself that I really do belong in college!" I actually had her repeat the last sentence because I couldn't believe what I was hearing. Didn't she recognize that she had worked her way through three and a half years of university with outstanding grades, had been chosen over others to serve in a demanding research assistant position, and had been picked to represent Heritage University at a prestigious intercollegiate event? And yet it was not until after all this that Louise finally could say to herself and to me that "I do belong in college."

If many first-generation students are like Louise, and I believe they are, then it is so important to employ strategies at the beginning of most courses that set a tone making students feel they are welcome, that they are equal participants with other students and the professor, and that they do belong in this class and at this institution. To do this, while also setting high standards and an expectation of hard work ahead, requires special planning. The approaches presented in this chapter are helpful resources to meet this chalenge.

CHAPTER 8

Relating to Students' Life Situations

IT WAS FRIDAY about two-thirds of the way through the term. Professor Jones looked out at his class made up primarily of commuter students who had shown a remarkable interest in his US History 102 class.

"Class, the first thing I'm going to do is collect the paper that is due today, the one about a person who interested you from the Civil War period that we've been studying. Please hand your papers to the end of the row so I can collect them."

As Professor Jones watched students hand their papers across the rows, he noticed a student in the second row who just passed the papers along without adding a paper of her own. He noticed because Tanya had been doing well in the class and had always handed in her work by the deadline. Not this time, he mused. After the class was over, he stopped Tanya on her way out of the room.

"Tanya, you didn't finish your paper for today?"

"No, Professor, I couldn't. Did you hear about the problem in the college's library last night? A water pipe or something. Well, they closed down the library at 5:00 and made everyone leave. So I couldn't work on my paper last night."

"I thought you told me yesterday morning that you had finished all your library research. Couldn't you have finished the paper last night?"

"I did have all the library research finished. But I still needed a couple of hours to write it all up and make it tie together."

"I'm really sorry you didn't get that done. You know you're going to lose a lot of points on this one coming in late. Couldn't you have finished it at home last night?"

"Write my paper at home?" Her voice got small and she shifted her gaze to the floor. "I don't think I could do that. I don't have a room to myself." Tanya's mind was racing as she thought, "My mom would flip out if I went to the bedroom and closed the door!"

Professor Jones was thinking, "Why not? I shared a room too but my kid brother always knew to leave me alone when I had to write a paper." But he thought better of saying any more. "Not good to pry into students' private lives," he thought.

After an awkward silence, he tried to say something positive: "Well, Tanya, your paper is late and you'll be losing those points on this one. So I'm sure next time you'll do a little better planning."

Tanya looked depressed. She was thinking, "How could I plan for the library having a flood?" She just stared again at the floor. After another awkward silence, the professor heard a mumbled, "I'll get it done as soon as I can," and watched as Tanya walked quickly to the door. He could only think of a lame response and called after Tanya, "See you next week."

WHAT'S GOING ON HERE?

Obviously, both Tanya and her professor are leaving this conversation with some discomfort. There are several factors at play here, and they are the basis for the communication mismatch that occurred. These include various aspects of Tanya's life experience that are different from her professor's. Neither of them is aware of what these factors looked like in the other's world. To begin with, Tanya and her family view college attendance with presumptions that are based primarily on her high school experience. She does not have family members who could share college-going experiences about professors and classes and homework expectations. In contrast, Professor Jones automatically pictures a family's involvement with their college student's needs. This was his own reality because of parents, siblings, and cousins who also had attended college, a different scenario from Tanya's family.

In addition, the physical setting of a working-class family's home and household, such as Tanya's, usually differs in significant ways from the middle-class professional family's household that Professor Jones experienced. While he may be slightly aware of these differences, it is unlikely that he has ever considered the implications of these variances and the practical consequences for Tanya as a college student living in her household. So let's unpack some of these unrecognized differences, and we may be able to understand more fully why their after-class encounter was unsettling to both of them.

Since Professor Jones is a caring and encouraging instructor, especially toward very promising students like Tanya, he is motivated to personally analyze this scenario. As he's driving home from the campus, he keeps asking himself what was going on in that short exchange with Tanya after class. In previous exchanges, Professor Jones had felt he was really able to connect with and encourage Tanya. In fact, they had discovered some similarities in their backgrounds, and that had created a kind of relaxed rapport when Professor Jones spoke with her about her research projects and previous papers. Both of them were born and raised in the same city. Tacitly they both recognized that they share the same ethnicity. These similarities, and Tanya's obvious interest in history, had created the expectation for Professor Jones that he could understand Tanya's needs as a student and respond helpfully to them, while holding her to high standards of work.

On Tanya's part, she thought Professor Jones would understand when she told him about the library's problem. Being required to leave the library obviously meant she could not stay at the only study spot she had found on campus, where she had planned to pull together the research information and complete her paper. Up until today she had felt that Professor Jones was a very understanding and supportive professor, which really motivated her to do her best in his class. But today he really didn't seem to care about her problems in meeting the deadline for this paper.

What neither Professor Jones nor Tanya knew and did not seem primed to recognize in this incident is something that can be a very significant factor in making or breaking communication incidents. There are actually significant cultural differences between them, in spite of the fact that both grew up in the same city, are from the same ethnicity, have a passion for the same subject of study (history), and currently are involved in a higher education setting. The two different subcultures they represent—college-going families and non-college-going families—form the basis for this cultural difference. This accounts for Professor Jones's lack of understanding about why a commuting college student from a working-class family could not complete an important homework assignment by the required date. His mental image and expectations are different from Tanya's and vice versa. As Lee Ward explains:

> Unfortunately, first-generation students receive relatively little cultural capital specific to higher education from their parents, who by definition have little or none of it to give . . . because their parents do not possess the information, familiarity, jargon, cultural understanding, experience, and emotional bearings that the students need to effectively tackle the challenges of the college environment.[1]

Because of this, Professor Jones was unaware that Tanya would have benefited from his guidance to help her deal with her life circumstances in relation to finding places to study effectively and to finish assignments on time.[2] This leads us to examine this incident in a little more detail.

When Professor Jones mentions that after Tanya was ejected from the library, she should have spent the evening completing her paper, his mental image is something like this. "I remember many times in college that I had to go into my room at home and do some serious writing. If my brother was in there on his bed, I'd make him be quiet, and I could get a lot done in there." If the professor had shared this silent reflection with Tanya, she might have only said, "Really?" and his response might have been, "Well, sure. My dad brought his accounting work home sometimes and went in their bedroom to get it done, and we got into trouble if we interrupted him." Tanya's likely response would have been, "Wow! My parents never bring work home." And Tanya would be thinking, "Of course they don't bring work home—my mom does housekeeping in the motel, and my dad does construction. How could they bring any of that home?" But even if the professor had shared his presumptions this explicitly, it's likely that she would be embarrassed about her parents' jobs, thinking that people with college educations are not usually construction workers and motel housekeepers. She would not be likely to explain why people in her household just don't bring their work home.

As we're becoming conscious of the mental conversations going on behind the verbal one, both at the conscious and at the pre- or unconscious levels, we see there are deeper issues at work here, from the viewpoint of social psychology and communication theories.[3] We have identified these in chapter 3 as communication mismatches. As we reviewed there, assumptions and expectations learned during the persons' socialization in their respective ethnicities, geographies, socioeconomic settings, genders, and various other microcultures are automatically operative for each one of them as an interaction proceeds. In the example we're exploring, the mental presumptions of the professor and the student differ widely, and we observe that even though each understood the literal meaning of the words that were used, a "match" in understanding did not occur. Being highly aware that this is possible in communication interactions with first-gen students is crucial for professors whose backgrounds are different from their students. To Professor Jones their different economic backgrounds—working class versus middle/professional class—didn't seem important in earlier conversations with Tanya, and he didn't see any need to know more about her home environment.

A mismatch occurs because of these unconscious presumptions about family living situations. For Tanya, those assumptions resulted in not asking for nor receiving guidance about her need to identify places to study outside of her home. And they resulted in Professor Jones being confused and mystified about why a student who seemed to be one of the stars of his class was not meeting a key expectation when she seemed to be right on track just a few days earlier.

This mismatch is more problematic because there are several matches also in effect. For example, both are aware that the next class session will begin in ten minutes, so their conversation will have to be brief, and both are also aware of the assignment that is under discussion. Each of them is making accurate assumptions about such things as whether both are comfortable speaking the same language and whether the ambient noise is so loud that one must speak louder than usual to be heard.

Professor Jones's unconscious assumptions about home living situations are shaped by growing up and currently living in a middle-class home environment where young adults each have their own room and all members of the family sometimes bring work from school or job to accomplish in a quiet place in the house. The accepted family norm is "don't disturb someone working on a writing or study project." In contrast, Tanya lives in a single-family dwelling currently occupied by members of both her immediate and extended family, making it a very crowded home. All of the adults in her house work at jobs that never entail bringing home any assignments requiring a quiet setting to think, compose longer written pieces, and/or calculate reports. None of the occupants has a bedroom to himself or herself. These significantly different unconscious scenarios of "home" influence the conscious assumptions that the professor and the student each make as the conversation progresses, producing very different understandings of such things as how much control the student has of her at-home, out-of-class time and whether she could find suitable study space in her home.

This example of "not having a place to do serious, quiet study" is only one of many life circumstances unique to a student from a first-gen, low-income family that often create barriers to becoming a successful college student. It is also only one of many life circumstances that may be entirely outside the unconscious mindset of typical professors, most of whom still come from college-going, middle-class families. Professor Jones's conversation with Tanya took him by surprise as it tapped into an unconscious assumption about home settings that he had never considered in this detail before. Now he worries that this incident might be indicative of personal and home issues that could directly affect the probability of Tanya's persevering and graduating.

When Professor Jones assigned a written paper he was focusing primarily on guiding students to find and use appropriate references and library resources as a preparation for the actual writing the student would need to do. He was thinking of that as the main challenge facing students as they tackled the writing assignment. Based on previous personal experience, he was visualizing the students writing their papers in similar circumstances to his own: in a residence hall room, curled up on the bed with a laptop or a notebook, or else bent over a small desk, laboring in a mostly quiet space to incorporate all the references gathered at the library. If Professor Jones had been a commuter student he might picture himself in a room at home with the door closed, or if no one else was home, working at a kitchen or dining room table. Perhaps his biggest challenge was turning off a favorite TV show while concentrating on writing, or ignoring a phone call from a pal or texts coming in on his cell phone.

Now switch to Tanya's world to see her unconscious assumptions at play while she talks to Professor Jones. Yes, she would have started out with a similar mental scenario to his—trying to find the right references and resources in the library, so she would have the material necessary to develop her paper. But once she is at the stage of writing it, her scenario as a first-generation, low-income commuter student changes dramatically from her professor's college-going experience. The idea of taking her library research materials home so she could work quietly by herself would never enter her head. She has learned by example and by admonitions from her parents and other adults close to her that being at home is a time and place to interact with and assist the family.

For instance, yesterday when she arrived home, the first thing she heard as she entered the house was, "Tanya, your baby brother needs help tying his shoes. And put a clean shirt on him for dinner. And hurry up—I'm just about ready to dish up the spaghetti." After dinner, she helped wash the dishes, and then was called to the front room to visit with her grandmother and her mother's half-sister who stopped by on their way back from the hairdresser. In no way can Tanya imagine saying, "Hi, Grandma and Aunt Rosie! Nice to see you. Sorry I can't visit tonight—I've got a really hard paper to write for college tomorrow. Bye for now. See you next time." Even if she had gotten up the courage to leave Grandma and Aunt Rosie in the front room, her non-college-going siblings would be likely to confront her later that evening with "Who do you think you are? You left Grandma and Aunt Rosie in the front room, like you were more important than they are! Mom is really mad at you."

On other occasions, when Tanya came home earlier in the day, she was expected to clean the younger children's room, or to call the light company to finagle an extension on paying this month's utility bill, and a dozen other homemaking chores. When Tanya's brother, who is also a commuting college student, arrives home, he can find himself assigned to paint out the graffiti that appeared on the back of the house recently, or to change the burnt-out lightbulb in the bathroom, or to mow the lawn, or any other of the "guy tasks" around the house.

With these close-up looks at Tanya and her brother's home setting, it becomes evident that first-gen students have a challenge that those of us with middle-class or professional-class backgrounds most likely have not had. Tanya and many New Majority students have to find other places outside the home, and dedicate other time, to do the demanding work of thinking in depth and writing good college papers. Once Professor Jones realizes this, he might ask himself, "Is this a challenge I could have anticipated? Could I help Tanya and other students successfully navigate these issues in the future?" And the answer is, "Yes!" Professors can make it part of their routine, as they begin a new class, to identify typical situations that their students are likely experiencing in their out-of-class time that could be barriers to success. They can mentally take a hypothetical walk through the scenarios that their students might have, and then identify potential predicaments students have to overcome in attempting to meet the class's requirements. In the incident we are examining, the professor could ask himself, "What would the scenario look like if Tanya had tried to work on her paper at home when the library was suddenly closed?" Even if she could have found a quiet place in the house, which appeared highly unlikely, she would probably be bombarded with questions. "Why aren't you helping with (fill in the blank)?" "Why didn't you do that work at school where it belongs?" "You think you don't have to help tonight and that you're better than the rest of us, just because you're going to college?" These are actual statements repeated to us at Heritage University by commuter students who tried at one time or another to work on a college assignment at home.[4]

BREAKING THROUGH THE BARRIERS CAUSED BY LIFE SITUATIONS

So what can concerned professors do to help first-generation commuter students like Tanya? The challenge is really one of changing student expectations and frames of reference. We are talking here about "time and space" issues. Two factors figure in this mind-opening process: identifying times to study and write papers, and finding appropriate space for completing college assignments.

Professors often presume that orientation programs provided by student services or admissions offices for their new students would have addressed the time and space factors by working on time management skills with students. Typical exercises used for orientation programs, such as those described in *The Secrets of College Success* (2nd Edition), by University of Arkansas professors Lynn Jacobs and Jeremy Hyman, are important and generally very helpful.[5] However, to be sure students do not see the time management portion of their "New Student Orientation Session" simply as theoretical and not really applicable to their daily lives as students, professors must change students' mindsets and assumptions about collegiate homework and the study required by helping them visualize how they will meet these requirements.

Creating Realistic Expectations About Personal Study Time

Before addressing the "space" or "place" problem with students, which we uncovered in Tanya's case, it is necessary to consider another underlying misconception in the mindset of most first-generation students. A second unconscious assumption on Tanya's part also played a role in her inability to meet the assignment deadline, leading her to leave the final writing of the paper until the last evening before it was due. It is the assumption that college courses are scheduled and homework is accomplished in approximately the same time frame and with a similar amount of attentiveness as in high school. With this inaccurate assumption Tanya is lacking knowledge of the amount of personal study time and effort required to complete a multipage analysis, and she therefore does not have an accurate sense of the individual planning that needs to take place in order to meet the deadline for the paper. Of course,

Tanya had to write some papers in high school, but those were shorter and probably didn't require the integration of research from a variety of different sources into the paper itself. In other words, they required neither as much time nor as much concentrated, uninterrupted effort to think ideas through and express them clearly in writing as a college paper requires. Also, in her public high school there was a study hall period assigned to her schedule, where quiet time and place were automatically provided. No such opportunities are included in a college student's assigned class schedule.

It is a generally unconscious expectation on the part of many first-gen students that college classes are basically just "much harder" high school classes, meaning that the only difference is that the ideas the professor will present are harder to understand.[6] Most first-gen students are from low-income families, and it is quite possible that they attended a public school that did not prepare students for the independent, rigorous, on-your-own study that university requires. Furthermore, there is no one in their homes to share stories of struggling through college classes, or to regale them with incidents of tough assignments, long papers, and being on your own to labor through course work. Many public high school teachers allow time during their class periods for students to get a good start on writing or reading assignments. In conjunction with their assigned study halls, these students subconsciously develop the expectation that they will be able to complete assigned papers during the school day. Recall that typically a high school student is scheduled into classes and supervised activities for about five to seven hours a day. It's a fairly big shock, especially for first-gen students, when they discover that they have only three or possibly four hours of scheduled class time on any given day, and that it does not include any assigned time in a designated study space, nor does it include any supervision or guidance on how to use effectively the remaining three to four hours of each school day.

At Heritage University I became acutely aware of how misunderstood the typical college course schedule could be several years ago when Joe, a first-gen commuter student, was assisted through the financial aid and registration process as a beginning freshman, but didn't show up for the first days of class. When a professor who had helped get him through the financial aid process saw him in the local grocery store a week or two later, she asked Joe why he was not attending. Joe answered, with embarrassment, that when his advisor gave him his schedule, he saw it had only morning classes. So he knew then that the advisor had realized he was not smart enough to take a regular load of classes because he did not schedule him for any classes in the afternoon. And that confirmed Joe's fear that he really wasn't capable of succeeding at college. So he figured it was better not to even start, rather than to set himself up for failure. What a shock to the professor and those of us who heard about that conversation!

It is certainly true that students whose parents and/or relatives have attended college still have the challenge of adjusting to the college schedule. But many have been hearing about the difference in college course work compared to high school for many weeks, months, and years preceding their arrival for the first day of college classes. Their parents, and perhaps older college-going siblings, aunts, or uncles, have regaled them with stories about what it is like to have "two hours of homework for every hour in class." They have probably heard examples of where and when these college-goers found time and place to give that kind of extended, focused attention to class assignments, like the need to spend Saturday in the library. Not so for the first-generation college students. Their only frame of reference is their high school classes, study halls, and activity schedules.

Guiding Students to Find Appropriate Study Space

Adding to the challenges created by their preconceptions about time, new college students who are commuters and from first-gen families face an additional challenge of finding and using appropriate places to study. This is reflective of a lack of awareness on the part not only of the students, but also of non-first-generation college staff and faculty. They simply don't realize that commuter students often need help solving not only the challenge of "time to study" but also the "place to study" dilemma.

Some successful first-gen students have found a good working space in the library as their primary refuge, but others have also identified alternate study areas such as a tutoring center, an academic success center, or an ethnic gathering space such as a Native American or Latino/a or African American center. Some have found a way to "hide out" in a corner of the dining hall or cafeteria, or to use a desk in a vacant classroom for an hour or two. However, many other first-generation students, especially those who drop out of college, report that one of their big problems was not having the time or a place to study.[7]

A very insightful catalogue of these and related needs of commuter, first-generation students is described by Professor Marcia Roe Clark, now at University of Massachusetts Amherst, in an article about urban commuter campuses. She concludes: "Fostering effective strategies includes making sure that students know about and access the campus resources [including study space] that can help them."[8]

Thus, the first step in helping first-gen students overcome this barrier of "time and place to study" is to help them prepare to be problem-solvers of their own "time and place" challenges. They must change their mental expectations, their mindset, about what it takes to be a successful college course-taker. Some professors assume that this task is the primary responsibility of the college orientation staff and make no plans within their course delivery to address students' misconceptions. In our experience, professors teaching freshman or sophomore first-generation students find that a greater percentage of their students complete assignments on time and earn passing grades if they start out the class with some kind of discussion and exercise to address this barrier of uninformed mental expectations. It is crucial to change the students' incorrect initial mindset about how much out-of-class study will be required and therefore how important it is to identify places and schedule times where they can successfully complete assignments.

Schedule Mapping

A useful approach is called the "schedule mapping" exercise. Give each student two blank preprinted templates, one labeled "High School Schedule" and the other "University [or College] Schedule." Sample templates may be found in the appendix at the end of this chapter. On the first one, have students fill in the blocks for a typical high school day from 8:00 a.m. to 5:00 p.m., showing what their daily and weekly schedule looked like during their last semester in high school. The template at the end of the chapter has Monday filled in, hypothetically, as an example. Have students fill in each one-hour block on the template with two pieces of information: the name of the class or activity, and the location where this took place. When the High School template has been filled in, have each student share it briefly with one other student, describing what he or she was doing and where he or she was doing it throughout a typical school day.

This helps students visually review what a typical school day has been in their experience to date and prepares them to recognize the contrast with their new college schedule. Next, have the students fill in the University template with their new college daily schedule, listing again for each hour both the activity they will engage in and where they will carry it out. Remind them, as they are filling in the template, of the principle that in universities two hours of study outside of every one hour in class is generally needed to meet the course requirements.

At this point in the exercise, Heritage University faculty have found it very useful to distribute to each student a campus map where he or she can locate personal study space. On the map, have the students identify the buildings or locations not only where their classes are held, but also where they might find quiet study space. Alternatively, rather than completing this during class time, you can assign students to investigate the map before the next class and bring back their recommendations for good places to study.

After students have completed filling out the second template, you can lead a general discussion on the students' observations about the differences between the two templates. At this point, it is generally easy to steer the discussion into the realities of how much personally scheduled study time each student is now responsible for, and the related dilemma of where this can be effectively undertaken. If you listen closely to students' comments, an added benefit for you is garnering information on their actual life situations, which will provide very helpful contexts for and greater understanding of future interactions with students who exhibit problems similar to Tanya's.

Further Practical Considerations

A caution is in order here. Most college classes have a mixture of first-gen students and those from college-going families. This can create a challenging environment in which to carry out the schedule mapping exercise described above, because of the difference in perceptions and expectations between the two groups. First-gen students are notorious for feeling "I'm not sure I belong here." They are consequently very sensitive to "looking stupid" in front of peers whom they perceive as "definitely belonging here."

In contrast, students from college-going families are often unaware of how much general knowledge about "the college experience" they have absorbed, mostly subliminally and over an extended period of time, from their parents and other college-going family members. They presume that all students will have the same general subliminal knowledge. The question that the schedule mapping exercise addresses of "where am I going to find study space for several hours every day outside class time?" is probably something they have already been led to think about, and may have received significant coaching about. Such students may find this exercise a bit condescending or too simplistic, and their candid reactions expressing that "this is a waste of our class time" during the discussion can inhibit students from non-college-going families from asking questions or making suggestions. It can also reinforce the first-gen students' perception that they aren't really adequately equipped to fit in and succeed in college. Professors need to keep an eye out for comments like these that may trigger embarrassment or silence from first-gen students.

An antidote to this awkward situation is a firm statement of support from the professor for the "creative" and "problem-solving" suggestions made by the first-gen students and, if appropriate, encouragement for them to share with the class the dilemmas they face in trying to study in their household. A short statement addressed to students who appear to disparage this exercise can take this approach: "The process of learning creative problem-solving is an important exercise for every college graduate to acquire, and if today's exercise didn't tap your creativity, I hope that a future challenging exercise will help unlock your creative problem-solving." Everyone values creative problem-solving, and this helps to legitimize the time spent on this exercise. Another helpful antidote is for the professor to share a story from his or her own life, or perhaps that of a sibling or cousin, which demonstrates challenges about study time and place that are similar, or comparable in significance, to those being experienced by first-gen students in the class. In this way, the "schedule mapping" exercise may help level the playing field between these two groups of students by focusing on each student's unique challenges.

A final step that helps students deal with the "place to study" challenge can be used during several of the follow-up class sessions. When you ask students a question about a completed homework assignment, add this to your question: "And also tell me where you did your work on this assignment." The answers that students give will provide additional potential options to other students as they listen to various responses. You will also get additional information about where and when students are actually studying, which may position you to give them some further helpful advice or encouragement as the term progresses.

ADDITIONAL RESOURCES

In this chapter, we have followed Professor Jones's discovery of an unexpected barrier to continued success for a student in his class, namely, her home situation as a first-generation student from a low-income family. At Heritage University, new professors usually discover early on for themselves, or from their seasoned colleagues, that a proactive approach regarding potentially difficult life circumstances for students is a smart move. At Heritage, with 85 percent of the students from first-gen families, engaging students in informal, friendly chats after class and around campus has been eye-opening and can introduce professors to life-circumstance challenges they had not imagined. However, for professors in most college settings, where less than 50 percent of the students are from first-gen families, this informal fact-finding may not be an efficient strategy, although it may produce other useful information about their students.

Fortunately, there are a number of very readable publications that can also expand a professor's awareness of problematic life situations for low-income and/or first-gen students that pose barriers to completing course work. For instance, Jere Brophy's book *Motivating Students to Learn* (2004) includes an analysis of why students are unmotivated and contains "useful treasure troves of information . . . dealing with motivating discouraged, uninterested, and alienated students."[9] Two of the four categories of "unmotivated" students identified by Brophy include students whose life circumstances are a key part of their motivational problems: those who have developed failure attributions and are experiencing learned helplessness, and those who are obsessed with self-worth protection due to negative reflections on their life circumstances from their more affluent, non-first-gen peers. Brophy's ideas about how to spark real motivation in students may offer useful insights for faculty.

Marcia Roe-Clark's articles on the unique challenges and problem-solving approaches of urban commuter students contain many revealing examples of situations experienced by first-gen students. These were gathered through an intensive qualitative research project with traditional-aged college freshmen at a commuter college. She reports, for example, that "urban commuter student success strategies can be highly inventive. They may lock themselves in a bathroom if that is the best place to steal some uninterrupted study time at home."[10] If I were hearing this strategy for the first time from a student, I might struggle to react in a positive and reinforcing way as I should, rather than with my spontaneous surprise and skepticism that might be off-putting and undermine the student's confidence. However, if I had read about this almost humorous yet practical strategy, as well as other unexpected challenges and solutions for first-gen students, it would be much easier for me to respond in supportive and encouraging ways.[11]

SUMMARY

This chapter has focused on specific unintended consequences of communication mismatches between typical university professors and their first-gen students. By carefully and fully unpacking similar scenarios as they occur in their own settings, professors have the opportunity to acquire new insights into barriers that inhibit these students. As more professors become attuned to this and other communication mismatch situations, they will enjoy a rewarding outcome: seeing more of their New Majority students flourish as they develop their talents, complete their college degrees, and become future community leaders.

TIME AND PLACE TEMPLATES

High School Time and Place Template

My High School Senior Year—Fall Term

		Mon Activity – Place	Tues Activity – Place	Wed Activity – Place	Thurs Activity – Place	Fri Activity – Place
8:00		English – Rm 101				
9:00		Chem – Chem Lab				
10:00		Aerobics – Gym				
11:00		W. History – Rm 201				
12:00		Lunch – Lunch Rm				
1:00		Algebra II – Rm 210				
2:00		Study Hall – Rm 112				
3:00		Debate Club				
4:00		Sports practice				
Evening		TV/cooking/dishes/ helping siblings with homework				

College Time and Place Template

My College Schedule for Classes, Study Time, etc.

	Mon Activity – Place	Tues Activity – Place	Wed Activity – Place	Thurs Activity – Place	Fri Activity – Place
8:00					
9:00					
10:00					
11:00					
12:00					
1:00					
2:00					
3:00					
4:00					
Evening					

CHAPTER 9

Reframing the Classroom as Community

PAUL WALKED OVER to the table in the dining hall where several of his class-mates were seated. They looked up at him with anticipation, because he was usually the life of the party. He always had some funny comment to make or a little joke to poke at one of them. But today he looked somewhat reserved or even downcast.

"Hey, Paul," one of the students called out. "Wha'dja think of class this morning? Professor Campbell was really wound up, wasn't he!" Paul didn't respond. He pulled up a chair and sat at the far end of the table, plopping his hamburger from the food line in front of him.

Another student chimed in. "It was kinda cool to hear what the professor read from some students' papers. Hey, I even got a couple of new ideas, hearing how some guys tackled that hard topic we had."

Paul's friend, Laura, was watching his uncharacteristically reserved behavior. "Wha'dja think when Professor Campbell read your paper, Paul? And when he posted it on the bulletin board?" She was goading him into some kind of response.

Paul looked up briefly from his hamburger and then looked down again. "Don't know if I'm even gonna write anything for the assignment he gave us for tomorrow." There was a quiet pause before Paul continued. "He didn't have to embarrass me in front of the whole class! Maybe he did that because I asked a question yesterday about the assignment and he wanted to get back at me."

Laura responded in a soothing voice. "Well, I'm sure glad it wasn't my paper he picked." She quickly added, "But you'll just have to get over it, Paul. It's the way college professors do things. I don't understand why they do that, but I guess that's the way it is in the university." The other students nodded as Laura spoke.

Meanwhile, faculty were coming into the other end of the dining hall from their morning classes, going through the cafeteria line, and sitting at nearby tables. Professor Campbell was sitting down to share his cafeteria lunchtime with some of his faculty friends. They greeted each other as they got settled. Professor Campbell took a couple of bites of his tuna salad sandwich before he decided to share his good feelings with his friends.

"Remember last week, when I was griping about my morning English class? Well, this morning I had a great session with them!"

The faculty member at his right smiled. "Glad to hear it. You were pretty discouraged with that group when you talked about them before."

Professor Campbell explained. "Maybe I picked just the right topic for their essay, but there were several good papers this time. It really made me feel better about this class."

Another professor asked, "So I'll bet you let the whole class know that, and they were glad to hear it."

"Yes, that's exactly what I did. I picked a few of the best papers and read parts of them to the whole class. They were all very quiet and seemed to listen intently. In fact, one paper—the student is Paul Sanchez—was so good that after I read it, I pinned it to the bulletin board so they could read the entire essay if they wanted to, and I gave him some real compliments. I was trying to give a good example to the other students that way."

"What a nice approach to rewarding a good piece of work," commented a third professor.

WHAT'S GOING ON HERE?

It's evident from the conversations at opposite ends of the dining hall that what took place in the morning English class has been understood in very different ways by the professors and by the students. And it's another classic example of communication mismatch. Professor Campbell thought that what he did in class was providing effective, positive reinforcement and encouragement to the students. The students, especially Paul Sanchez, whose paper he put on the bulletin board, interpreted Professor Campbell's actions in a way he never intended. If we tried to tell Professor Campbell that he embarrassed Paul by posting his paper, his response might be, "Of course he's a little bit embarrassed. Young people are like that. But he is secretly feeling lots of pride and he'll be really motivated to keep improving his writing." And that would miss entirely what is actually going on with Paul and his student companions. Paul and his friends are not simply feeling that he was embarrassed a little bit in front of his peers. They are not taking this as something they will easily ignore and then move on to other topics. They seem to share Paul's perception that the professor's actions put him in an intensely uncomfortable and undesirable position.

For those of us experienced in an American academic milieu, we might expect Paul's friends to continue embarrassing him about Professor Campbell's actions, in a teasing manner similar to what we see football players doing to a teammate right after he has successfully run many yards, taking the ball into the end zone and scoring a touchdown. The teammates are often seen punching him, or jumping on him, or slapping him, actions that cause some immediate pain. But we know these are being used to communicate the opposite sentiments, namely admiration and respect. We might ask ourselves, isn't Paul's reaction of embarrassment normal for young people when they are recognized for an accomplishment, as Professor Campbell thought? And won't his classmates continue ribbing him a bit? The answer is "No," and that becomes clear when we hear the rest of the students' comments. They obviously don't see Paul's experience as something desirable or helpful.

What is at the root of the significantly different understandings of the same classroom scenario by the professors and the students?

One way to explain this is that there are two dissimilar underlying values operating here. These values have to do with what an individual has been raised to believe are appropriate reasons for working hard to achieve success. Each sociocultural group communicates to its young people distinctive rationales regarding the primary motivations and goals that a person should espouse. At either end of a spectrum are two contrasting value systems, which have been identified in research by Professor Nicole Stephens and her colleagues as "independence" versus "interdependence."[1] These are especially relevant when we look at the college milieu through the eyes of students.

On the one hand, when Professor Campbell was a student, he learned from his middle-class family and friends that it is desirable and appropriate to be recognized as an individual, to be your own person in thought and action, and to develop an individual path toward success in life. If you do this, you will feel satisfaction with yourself and your efforts, and your family will be proud of you and feel they have been effective in raising you. This underlying motivation or personal value is what is meant by the label "independence." I referred briefly in chapter 1 to the extensive research Professor Nicole Stephens and her colleagues conducted about this concept in relation to first-gen students at four different universities (Northwestern University, Stanford University, University of Arizona, and San Jose State). They identified the effects of contrasting underlying motivations between middle-class and working-class students in regard to their success in completing degrees. They saw this issue as significantly affecting working-class students' feelings of belonging in their college or university. From their research, they describe the "independence" motivation this way:

> For people socialized in American middle-class environments, college is not only an expected part of the life plan; it is the ultimate symbol of independence. When transitioning from one's home to the university, students are led to believe that they will finally be able to separate and distinguish themselves from their parents and to realize their individual potential—to find themselves, to develop their voices, to follow their passions, and to influence the world.[2]

On the other hand, the motivation that these researchers identified and called "interdependence" is typical of working-class students like Paul Sanchez and his friends. They have been socialized to focus on the importance of community and family as the primary motivation for working hard. Young people from this sociocultural group usually learn that one's top priority is assisting one's family and community to be better materially, emotionally, or physically. Many students from continuing-gen, middle-class backgrounds will also recognize the altruistic aspect of this approach as an important value learned in their families. However, for them it is generally regarded as a desirable outcome that will occur if one focuses first on being successful in gaining personal independence and self-directedness, along with achieving new levels of knowledge and competence. This will in turn make the individual both successful and capable of choosing to make a difference in the community. This difference in initial focus between the independence motivation and the interdependence motivation is a significant factor that can be alienating for students coming from communities that value interdependence, because the typical academic culture reflects the independence value of middle-class, continuing-gen students who have formed the main student body in universities during the past several generations. Professor Stephens and her colleagues found that adjusting to the dominant university culture of "independence" creates some challenges to a healthy sense of belonging for "students with working-class backgrounds, who are likely to have been socialized with different rules of the game—rules that do not emphasize independence but instead emphasize interdependence, including adjusting and responding to others' needs, connecting to others, and being part of a community."[3]

For first-gen students from low-income families, especially those from many ethnic minority groups, the emphasis on community over personal needs is so strong that the young person has been trained to always be aware of the needs of those around him or her and to meet those needs whenever possible. This person feels satisfied and motivated to continue trying when the community and/or family are benefiting from the person's actions. Professor Stephens and her colleagues explain the interdependence orientation's effect on most New Majority students:

Although first-generation students may recognize independence as the American cultural ideal, their prior experiences in their local working-class family and community contexts are likely to have been guided mainly by norms of interdependence . . . As a result first-generation students are likely to experience the university culture's focus on independence as a cultural mismatch— as relatively uncomfortable and as a clear divergence from their previous experiences.[4]

Identifying these two differing motivational mindsets helps us to unpack the divergent conversations at either end of the cafeteria. On the one hand, Professor Campbell believes he will provide extra motivation to his students if he calls out the success of individuals, either by reading sections of their papers aloud, or by posting the best essay on the bulletin board for everyone to see. This is based on his own personal experience and that of many of his peers. Growing up middle-class with parents and other relatives who had earned college degrees, he experienced praise and feeling good about himself and successfully in tune with his college when his individual work was singled out and recognized as outstanding.

On the other hand, his student, Paul, feels penalized and is demotivated by having his paper read aloud and then exhibited in a public place with a high grade and compliments written on it. Why? Because he has learned from his family and community that to be singled out individually and recognized separately from one's family or community is selfish, egotistical, and shows a lack of loyalty toward one's family and community. Those who are singled out as individuals in public may be subsequently shunned or ridiculed at home, and Paul certainly wants to avoid that.

This story reminds me of an incident some years ago with a new faculty member at Heritage University. She had a distinguished career in her subject area and had taught at several East Coast institutions when life circumstances brought her to the Pacific Northwest and Heritage. She had a very pleasant personality and I had observed that students seemed quite comfortable around her outside of class. She approached me one day after class to say that she was exasperated and completely baffled by something a student had told her earlier in the day. I'll call him Jon.

Two weeks earlier she had posted Jon's excellent paper, marked with an A and complimentary notes, on the bulletin board in her classroom. Then a few days ago she posted two other students' excellent papers from the second assignment. She had noted that Jon had not submitted the second paper, which was puzzling since his first paper was so good and she had given it special recognition. On the day the professor was speaking with me, she had stopped Jon as he entered the classroom and asked if he had finished the second paper yet, since it was now three days overdue. He responded that he was not going to hand in any other papers for her class. When pressed for a reason, he shared that his two cousins who also attended Heritage had seen his earlier A paper on the bulletin board and had asked why he was showing off and embarrassing his family. When the professor looked surprised and puzzled at this comment, Jon added that in his family, "it just isn't right to be singled out. It's . . . it's rude to the rest of your family and relatives." So Jon said he had decided not to hand in any more papers for her class so they couldn't be posted.

The professor then asked him why he was still coming to class if he wasn't going to do the writing assignments. He answered that he really liked the subject area and wanted to continue learning about it, and he enjoyed the class discussions. He was planning on perfect class attendance and good test performance and he figured that would enable him to pass the class. The professor, not surprisingly, was taken aback again. She saw his behavior as confusing and counterproductive but didn't know how to proceed with him.

While I had never heard a story quite this dramatic about first-gen students' aversion to having their exemplary work singled out for individual praise, I had become aware of the communication mismatch underlying this incident. So I explained to the professor the norm under which this student was raised and currently lived, and advised her to tell him that she had decided not to post any more papers, so he could safely submit subsequent assignments. A few weeks later I learned that this strategy had solved the problem. The student continued to contribute positively to class discussions, he submitted the remaining written assignments, and completed the course with a strong B grade.

It was only several years later that I read the research by the professors working with Professor Nicole Stephens and learned the very descriptive designations for the two contrasting value systems, independence and interdependence, quoted in part above.

REFRAMING CLASSROOM ROUTINES

The first step for professors who want to motivate and make first-gen students feel they belong in college and in this class is to thoroughly understand the underlying basis for the interdependence value system and begin to think about ways of reframing classroom routines that tap into the student's desire to support community. When you think about it, this value system makes a lot of sense in most of the communities where low-income students live. This is because it is a logical approach to dealing with living situations characterized by very limited resources in one's own family and community. People living in such neighborhoods or rural residence areas not only have few resources personally; they also depend upon sharing among family members or close neighbors. These areas generally have few other community resources within easy reach, such as good transportation options, robust financial institutions, well-stocked local grocery stores, drop-in clinics, and other supportive resources that depend upon a good tax base. These under-resourced areas are often characterized by higher property crime rates, and families living there rarely have relatives or extended family living elsewhere in more affluent regions who can share resources with them. In this environment, placing the highest value on loyalty to and active responsibility for one's community makes sense. It results in young people being held accountable first of all for the well-being and safety of their family and community. They learn to use this mindset as the primary way to think of themselves and their interactions with others. This creates a different mental map than the one that emerges when a young person is regularly encouraged to become a "shining star," or to step up and "do it on your own," or to be responsible for "developing your own talents so your parents will be proud of you."

Faculty from middle-class backgrounds teaching mostly continuing-generation students may never have had occasion to consider the interdependence value system in relation to classroom interactions, until they experience serious reticence on the part of students to have their work used as an example of excellence or to be asked to present alone in front of the entire class. These occasions put the interdependence value system in a negative light for college success. I referred earlier to detailed research on this topic, and you might find helpful information about implications of the interdependence motivation for New Majority students in the full article in the *Journal of Personality and Social Psychology*.[5]

After considering the downsides of the interdependence motivation mindset, it is refreshing to look at it in a different light. The interdependence value is actually an untapped resource available to professors who are teaching primarily first-generation, low-income students. Below we'll explore several ways that professors can make this mindset work favorably for both students and professors.

Reframing Attendance

Professor Elese Washines at Heritage University has developed a unique way of reframing the topic of attendance as an important way for students to help themselves as well as their classroom peers. She points out to students that they are joining a community by becoming members of this class. She has them look around the room and note that they will be with these twenty-five (or whatever number) fellow students for thirty gatherings of ninety-plus minutes during the next four months. She points out that any time you spend that many hours over an extended period with the same group of people, you are in a community. As a member of this community, you share responsibility for your fellow classmates. If you are not in class one day, it makes the other students question why they are there. If you are not there, you might have been the one person in the class who would have asked a crucial question that would have helped everyone else understand a difficult concept, and thereby, you have let down your classmates. By signing up for this class, you have become partially responsible for your classmates, and they share a responsibility for you. You are all in this together!

When Professor Washines uses this approach, she is tapping into a basic standard of behavior from these students' families and communities—interdependence—which these first-gen, low-income students have learned and live by. She has a special advantage as she describes this, because she is an active member of the Yakama Nation, where the importance of thinking of yourself first of all as a member of this community is a long-standing, sociocultural norm for the Yaka-mas. But Elese reports that she receives very responsive reactions from the non-Native, first-gen students in the class, too. Their experiences in working-class families in low-income neighborhoods, or as members of immigrant families, have fostered the value they place on community. When she makes this pitch to the class, she observes that it energizes something within these students, making them feel a new commitment to this class and a new sense of belonging. This is especially important for first-gen students for whom a sense of belonging is often missing as they attempt to become successful college students.[6] As we explored in the previous two chapters, helping New Majority students feel that they belong is a major challenge for professors. Professor Washines also reports, as do several other faculty who have adopted her approach, that class attendance improves significantly when she uses this method of talking about regular attendance, and she continues to mention this throughout the term. Most professors, including those at Heritage University, report that regular attendance is one of the best predictors of passing the course.[7]

Getting Responses to Questions

Another unanticipated result of presiding over a class with many first-gen students may be the difficulty of figuring out how to overcome their stubborn reticence to volunteer an answer to questions that the professor throws out to the entire class. In the traditional college scenario in the memory of most middle-class professors, after fellow college students had read a chapter assigned at the previous class session, they expected their professor to throw out questions about the reading to the entire class; volunteering to answer and being called on was an important way to gain the confidence of the professor and prove that you had done the reading. So when this former student, now a professor, faces the class after giving them a reading assignment in the previous session, he or she generally has prepared a series of questions to throw out to the class. The professor expects various students to raise their hands, anxious to be called on so they can demonstrate that they did the reading. When almost no one in the class, or only the same few (probably continuing-gen) students, will raise their hands and respond to the questions, it is hard for the professor not to be frustrated and a bit irritated.

A Heritage University professor of philosophy, Sister Michel Keenan, IHM, whose previous long experience at Marywood University in Pennsylvania had made her an expert in developing thought-provoking questions, experienced this frustration and mystifying reaction when she first came to Heritage University. As she became aware of the community and interdependence values influencing her first-gen students at Heritage University, that led them to resist volunteering answers, she soon developed a very successful approach to overcoming this difficulty. She prepared in advance the same number of questions as the number of students in the class, and she told the students in advance that every student would receive a question to answer regarding the assigned reading. Since all students knew that everyone else in the class would be responding orally to a question, they no longer felt that they would be uncomfortably singled out. It was a predictable part of being the "team" in this class. While individual confidence or shyness or poor preparation was still evident as various students responded to their individual questions, the earlier firm unwillingness of almost all the class members to "put myself out front" disappeared.

There are various ways to use this "question-for-each-student" approach. One way is to print the questions, cut them into individual slips of paper with only one question per slip, and have students draw one out of an envelope or basket. After everyone has a question, let individuals volunteer to answer, while someone keeps track of who has answered and who has not, so every person must answer a question sooner or later. Another way is to call on students in alphabetical order, asking each one to answer the question he or she drew.

Once students are used to this "one-student, one-question" way of reviewing an assigned reading, the professor can further build their confidence and courage in being able to answer questions in front of the class by not passing out the questions to each student ahead of time. Use a list of students to call on each one and pose a question that he or she must answer. Or let students volunteer when they are ready to hear your next question and give their answers.

Professors can develop other approaches to implementing this approach of arranging for each student in the class to have equal responsibility for answering review questions, thus honoring the teamwork/interdependence orientation that many first-gen students bring with them to college.

Group Work = Teamwork

Professors today are generally well informed on the usefulness of group work as a means of getting students engaged more fully in their own learning. Connecting what we already know about group work with the New Majority student priority on interdependence requires some adaptations in the usual group work scenario. The key is creating an experience of *teamwork* within the group work structures. There are two common complaints from students about group work. The first, observed by both student participants and many professors, is that only one or two students in the group are really involved and always dominate, while others in the group do not learn as much because they are not really engaged. The second complaint is an entirely different one and may come as a surprise to some. This is the complaint from some New Majority students, documented by Simon Fraser University's Professor Rebecca Cox, who finds that these students often mistakenly believe that a professor who puts students into discussion groups is doing so only to avoid having to present information and do the teaching he or she is supposed to do.[8] They see it as a sign that the professor is shirking his or her duties rather than an important way to provoke deeper learning and retain meaning in a subject. With this misunderstanding by students, Professor Cox documented that group work often devolves into chatting about their social lives or other topics unrelated to the current subject in the class.

How can group work be structured so that these two pitfalls are avoided? Here are some criteria that usually are effective in overcoming the two complaints described above.

1. Keep the groups small, usually between three and five when significant discussion topics are included in the group assignment. This makes it harder for group members to remain uninvolved.

2. Give an explicit description of why you are asking the students to participate in group work. Include these two points: A) Tell them that your experience, as well as research on how students learn, has taught you that they will actually be able to answer questions on the current subject with greater depth and accuracy after they have participated in the upcoming group exercise, than if you spent the same amount of time talking at them about this subject.[9] B) Remind them that they are in a community of learners and that their small group is a "team" in which each of them is responsible to see that everyone in the group participates and is learning.

3. Design the small group assignment so that there are several distinct roles for individual students to fill. If there are not enough roles to match the number of students in the typical group, plan the group process so that everyone has to assume one of the roles at some time. The main goal is to guarantee through the explicit details of the group process that each student will have a distinctive task to fulfill. By doing this, you eliminate the possibility that a student can remain entirely passive and only be a listener (or daydreamer) during the whole small group process.

Here is an example of one way to organize the small group work. This process can be applied in a variety of classes where you have assigned an article for reading or a chapter of a text or other book. Rather than simply having students discuss an article or chapter in their group, give them this process and walk them through it.

STEP 1: Assign reading of the whole article or chapter before class. Or, if it is only one or two pages in length, have the group quietly read the entire article individually once they are in their group.

STEPS 2 AND 3: Identify two key paragraphs and tell the group to pick two readers who will each read one of the paragraphs aloud, after everyone has finished reading the entire piece silently.

STEP 4: Tell the groups that their job, which they will report to the entire class at the conclusion of the group time, is to pick the idea that their group believes is the most important one in the entire article. Tell them that they are working as a team, and everyone's best participation is necessary for their team to shine when the report-back time comes. To start, each group member is to write down what he or she thinks is the most important idea in the article. (This can also be structured to write down the two or three most important ideas in a chapter or article.) Give them several minutes to fulfill this step quietly.

STEP 5: Then have all students pass their papers with what they think is the most important idea(s) to the next person, who reads it and writes any comments on the paper. They continue passing the papers around, reading and commenting, until all group members have seen and commented on all papers. At that point the group can begin a discussion together to decide on what their team believes to be the most important idea in the article.

STEP 6: Next, call them all back together again to hear the conclusion from each team, and identify which team produced the best answer. If there is some reward for the team that produced the best answer, such as giving the winning team a few extra points toward their grades, or designating them to be the first team that gets to report next time, or some other recognition, students usually will experience feeling good about their team, or if they were not the winners, a desire to be the winning team next time. This sparks additional energy and focus for students.

This example of a small group structure for class work capitalizes on the first-gen students' priority for community loyalty and involvement in team success. This approach will also appeal to many continuing-generation students, especially as the emphasis on team sports identity at colleges and universities continues to grow. It turns the interdependence community value into an asset for student involvement rather than a liability. In addition, it requires every student to be involved individually. Professors can structure many other templates of successful small group teamwork plans to achieve these same outcomes, if they avoid explicit reference to individual independence motivations and consciously employ interdependence approaches.

Anticipating Pushback

We have been examining student attitudes in the classroom that flow from a core value common among New Majority students that emphasizes community. When we combine this insight that affects classroom interactions with the day-to-day situations experienced by students whose parents never attended college, we see a need for some direct actions that address the issues students are experiencing because of these combined realities. Periodically these students experience real pushback from their families in regard to some aspect of college involvement that families think is unnecessary or irrelevant to their student's success and a burden to the family. For instance, if students are participating in a specially funded program for New Majority students, they may be asked to attend a noncredit workshop on a topic like time management or budget planning, or to attend a technical seminar such as how to use the search engines on the university's library website. If the required or highly recommended sessions are scheduled at a time when the commuter student usually is participating in some family-serving activity such as a grocery shopping trip or a previously scheduled family meal, the mother may say, "That's not part of the class schedule you showed me, so why are you choosing that over your family responsibility?"

To help students deal with this type of question from family members, since it is unlikely that they will bring up their dilemma in class, professors can be proactive whenever they assign or suggest an activity that will require the student to be available during previously unscheduled time. Some examples of occasions when professors can anticipate potential family pushback include

- visiting lecturers at the university who are making public presentations in subjects very appropriate to the student's class or major;
- workshops or seminars provided by the tutoring or academic success center to help students improve on skills the professor has noted are weak or lacking;
- student club meetings or activities of a club that relate directly to the class or the students' major;
- extended lab times that may be open-ended, due to unpredictability of the planned experiments;

- required group time outside of class to fulfill certain assignments; and
- presentations by other students in more advanced classes in this major, where they will share the results of their research or their project reports.

Let's look at how a professor might be helpful in these circumstances. Usually, students will be reticent to volunteer information about negative feedback they are receiving from family members. But they may be willing to open up a bit if the professor broaches the topic by sharing something he has heard from a previous student or something he has read. Here's a possible classroom strategy:

> "Class, you know that I am strongly encouraging you to attend the seminar presentation by the seniors in our department next Thursday at 4:30 p.m. I really hope you all can come. I don't know if any of you might be having a problem with family obligations that would interfere with being able to attend this seminar.
>
> "I remember reading recently about a student whose parents didn't have any college experience. When she told her mother that she would not be able to be present when her aunt and family were coming over for a special dinner because she had to go hear a visiting lecturer, her mother got quite upset. She told her daughter, 'We're already supporting you in your choice to go to school instead of getting a job and working. Now you're telling me you won't be part of the family for this special event that we've had planned for a long time, just because someone is giving a talk at the university? What's happening to your loyalty and concern for your family?' I wonder if any of you think you might hear anything like that, or anything else problematic, from your family if you tell them that you are going to this Seminar and won't be home during that time?"

Ideally, at least one student will respond to your question and either share what he or she has heard at home, or at least heads will nod in agreement with you that something negative might be said. This opens the door to do some strategizing with students about how to handle these situations.

Here are several points that faculty at Heritage University have shared with us about how they help students deal with this challenge.

- Encourage students to initiate a conversation about the upcoming opportunity with the family member likely to be offended *before* announcing that the student will not be home at that time.
- Tell students to start by explaining in as much detail as they can about what a useful and worthwhile opportunity this is.
- Ask the students if they feel competent to describe specific details of this event and why it is worthwhile. If not, do some brainstorming with them to surface as many positive reasons and details as possible.
- Tell students that only after giving a full explanation of the event and the details of its importance should the student say something like, "I really believe it's important for success in my [class / major / with my advisor] for me to attend this, and I really don't want to offend anyone if I miss this [family event]."
- Suggest this final argument: "This [event] is already paid for as part of the charges for this term, and you would want me to take advantage of everything we have already paid for."

If most of the students in a given class appear to be New Majority scholars, setting aside ten or fifteen minutes during class to do the above five-step exercise will be well worth the time, and this probably has to be done only once during the term. If more students attend the recommended event because of this strategy, it is definitely a worthwhile exercise.

Continuing-generation students in the class may feel this discussion is a waste of time, and if they are a significant part of the class enrollment, here's a tweak to this strategy. Give a short speech similar to the one on the previous page that opened the topic and then tell students that if anyone would like to discuss how to handle similar situations in their own lives, you will meet with those interested students either fifteen minutes before or fifteen minutes after the next class. In this way, you will reach the New Majority students who need this supportive and proactive help from you, but you will not make the continuing-generation students feel you are misusing their class time.

SUMMARY

Stepping back and taking a big-picture look at the interdependence or community motivation of New Majority students leads us to the conclusion that this is a value system that will benefit our future society as a whole. Therefore, we need to employ strategies that capitalize on this value while helping students learn to become active, successful college students. With their college degrees under their belts and their strong priority on interdependence intact in their value system, they will be poised to become strong and effective leaders of our society in the global village of the future.

PART THREE

STRATEGIES TO ENGENDER CONFIDENCE

PROFESSORS NEED to be aware that the task of building students' confidence will require some different approaches with first-generation students than with most continuing-generation students. Working to build a first-generation student's confidence requires the professor to say and do appropriate things over a much longer time frame and with more frequent reinforcing comments.

Moreover, building confidence needs to be combined with maintaining high standards for student performance. This reality creates extra challenges for professors working with first-generation students whose confidence level may be low. Those with extra-low confidence can lose hope and the motivation to keep trying if their initial efforts are unsuccessful. Finding ways to motivate these students to try again, and then gradually to reinforce the slowly increasing confidence of New Majority students, step by step, creates the need for professors to seek out or create classroom strategies that build confidence. The strategies described in this section include explicit approaches and discussions faculty can have to bridge cultural differences and build confidence in their students. These strategies include exploring the challenges that come with doing something new, incorporating journal writing into the class requirements (including faculty responses to individual journal entries), and helping students surface and develop their own original ideas.

CHAPTER 10

Creating Confidence

A Professor's Role

THREE ENVIRONMENTAL SCIENCE STUDENTS *gathered around Professor Miller after the other students had left the lab. "Thanks for staying for a few minutes," she opened the conversation. "I've just learned about a great opportunity, and you are the three best students to take advantage of it. That's why I asked you to stay after lab so I can see if you are willing to be involved."*

The students looked intently at her, their reactions appearing to be either expectant interest or a fearful pulling back. She continued. "The State Department of Forestry just contacted me because of the project we did with them last summer in the wildfire area off White Pass. They're having a meeting with other forestry people from Oregon, Idaho, and Montana in a few months, and they would like to have some of our students present reports on our project."

Marie, the student with the excited look on her face, reacted. "Wow! They're asking for us to give some reports, and not our professor?"

Professor Miller smiled. "Well, I think that shows they were really impressed with what you students did, how involved you were, and how committed you were to the project's goal. I'm very proud of you, that they are inviting you to speak."

"So do they want one student to report or a couple of us?" Marie asked.

"They want one student to report on the preparations and rationale that went into our accepting to work with them on this project. Then they want a second student to describe what our team of ten students actually did while we were out there with the forestry professionals. And they are asking for a third person who would report on what we're learning from our analysis of the information and data we brought back. So I picked the three of you as the students on our team who will best represent us."

Since Marie had been the only one to express interest so far, Professor Miller turned to the other two students. *"Robert and Cristina, what do you think? Would you be willing to work on preparing these presentations?"*

Robert responded first. *"I don't think I could do that. I—I just couldn't put together a presentation like that and deliver it in front of all those forestry professional people. That's just not me. I think I told you when we were out there this summer that my dad sometimes works for the Forest Service on some of the clean-up crews. That's when there's not work in the fruit orchards or the hay fields. I think a lot of those forestry guys know my dad, and they wouldn't think I could be up there talking to them like I know something they don't. Besides, I don't want to act like I think I'm better than my dad. No way!"*

Cristina had been looking at the floor, but when Robert finished, she spoke up, quietly but firmly. *"Professor, it's really nice of you to ask me, but do you remember what I told you about my high school counselor? I know you didn't agree with him, but he knew me for four years, and you've only known me for less than two! I think he was probably right."*

Professor Miller looked a little frustrated. *"Chris, I remember you shared with me that your high school counselor said something about you're not being college material and wanted you to go to the technical school, but I've told you before that I don't believe he was right. You've gotten very good grades so far, and you were really creative and smart about the data gathering we were doing this summer. You can do it!"*

Marie interrupted this conversation to say, *"Well, I would be really excited to do that, Professor. I'm going to say 'Yes' right away. I have to go to my next class, though. Can we talk about it more next week after class?"*

"Of course we can, Marie." Professor Miller patted Marie on her shoulder as she left the room. Then she turned back to Robert and Cristina.

"Well, Marie thinks she can do one of the reports, and she isn't any better than the two of you in her class work or lab projects. All three of you get mostly A's. It should encourage you to know that Marie will be working on this!"

Robert looked away and said, "But there's a big difference, Professor. Marie's father is an attorney. Every now and then she'll mention some unusual case he's working on. She gets to hear her own dad talk about preparing reports and presentations! No wonder she's willing to try it, too. That just isn't my family, and I'm not sure it's me."

After a pregnant pause, Professor Miller took a deep breath and said, "Well, I hear both of you saying that you would like to say 'No' to my request. Will you please do me a favor, and keep an open mind until next week? We can talk about it more then. Keep reminding yourselves that I have confidence you both can do this or I wouldn't have picked you out of the class."

As Professor Miller turned back toward the lab tables, Robert and Cristina nodded, still looking unsettled, and murmured a quiet "Bye" as they walked out of the room.

WHAT'S GOING ON HERE?

Every professor with any experience in the classroom has undoubtedly encountered the problem of students' lack of confidence. This is a problem that we encounter with both first-generation and continuing-generation students. Like many issues of personal feelings and attitudes, different individuals experience these for a variety of reasons, and there is not just one simple explanation. In attempting to change these interior states of mind, you can be much more effective if you have accurately discerned the root causes for an individual's particular mental state at issue and employ strategies that can bridge cultural divides, build relationships, and ultimately boost student confidence.

For first-generation students, there are several root causes for a lack of self-confidence in academic settings. In Professor Miller's interaction, Robert demonstrated quite explicitly one of those root causes. Coming from a strong family experience, there is a profound reticence to take on a new role, especially in a public setting, that is significantly beyond anything that his parents and elders have done. Robert is not at all comfortable with stepping into the role of a presenter at a gathering of professionals because he knows his own father lacked the educational background to ever do anything like that. He is facing a double-edged mental sword: in addition to not having any helpful input at home that might assist him to succeed in this task, he is also aware that he may be seen by his family members as trying to outshine his dad, thereby demonstrating his father's lack of achievement—a very rude and uncaring thing for a good son to do.

It may be hard for Professor Miller to picture Robert's internal struggle, because the mainstream culture in America places a high value on parents encouraging their children to go beyond their own level of accomplishment and to achieve a more advanced level of education or financial success or professional recognition. Many low-income families also give this encouragement to their children. But in some cultures, apparently including Robert's, the importance of respecting and valuing one's parents is coupled with the tacit understanding that loyal, good youth will try to follow in their parents' footsteps and do as well or perhaps a little better than their parents, but not step into entirely new roles.

This point was very poignantly brought home to me one time in a conversation with a young man on campus who was a senior and expected to graduate at the end of the year. I was praising him for getting to this stage and he stunned me by responding, "I don't think I can go through with the rest of this year and be in graduation. I just don't feel right getting a college degree when my father didn't get one and never had a chance to." Of course I tried to talk him out of this conclusion, and he did finish the fall term, but he did not re-register in the spring and so did not graduate. Fortunately several of his professors kept hounding him, and he finally came back to finish the remaining courses and earn a degree. He told one of them that when he finally admitted to his father why he wasn't finishing his degree, his dad had told him, "I know you think you're doing that for me, son, and I know I have complained over the years about how I never had the opportunity to go to college. But if you finish that degree, now I will be so proud of you and I will be able to tell others that I have a son with a college degree."

In Robert's case, this pressure seems especially relevant because his father occasionally works for the same forestry people who will attend the presentation that Robert is being asked to give. Robert appears to be coming either from a more traditional cultural upbringing or perhaps from a chronic-poverty setting. If Robert and/or Cristina come from a multigenerational poverty setting, the lack of hope or expectation that things can change often forms the family's dominant approach to reality. Parents who have lived their entire lives with this mental map of their family's and ancestors' reality may profoundly wish that this could change, but they have never seen or heard of it happening, and have no hope of seeing it in their lifetimes. So they are reticent to encourage their children to try something outside the expected realm of possibility because they don't want to see their children fail and be hurt and deeply disappointed. If this is the case for Robert or Cristina, it appears that they have already pushed the envelope by enrolling in college. But, even if they might be tempted to take on the challenge being offered by the professor, it would take a great deal of courage and energy to keep at bay the strong belief they experience at home that "our people don't do those things."

There may also be some peripheral issues related to a low-income lifestyle that don't occur to the professor. These include not having professional-style clothing to wear to the event in question, or not knowing what kind of attire is expected and being embarrassed to ask about it. Transportation is also sometimes an issue, although in this case the way to get to an off-campus site was obviously solved for the students during their summer work together. Professors who take a pro-active approach to these practical barriers will find that simple things like arranging for appropriate clothing will sometimes have a significant positive effect on students' confidence.

Turning to the continuing-generation student in the opening scenario, Marie, we see that she already has the confidence to take up the opportunity that Professor Miller presented. But there are many continuing-generation students who would not have been as eager as Marie to take on this new challenge. They, too, can suffer from a lack of confidence. Dr. Carol Dweck of Stanford University has led the way in helping us to understand why this happens with young people, especially those raised in the last half of the twentieth century, and perhaps especially those who are raised by well-educated parents. The most popular child-rearing publications of that era stressed the importance of praising children as they grow up. What that literature did not explain, perhaps because it was not known to the authors, was that all praise is not the same. What praise is given for makes a very big difference in what effect it has on the young person. Dweck's research has shown that when praise is given for "being smart" rather than for "working hard" or "trying different ways," individuals begin to believe that they have a fixed amount of intelligence that is a key part of who they are. Consequently, they become fearful to try anything unknown or extra difficult because if they aren't successful, it would show that this key part of who they believe themselves to be is actually false. As Dweck explained to the interviewer Sujata Gupta for the *Proceedings of the National Academy of Sciences of the United States of America,* "We found that the students who were praised for their intelligence did not want to take on a challenging task afterward. They wanted to play it safe. When we did give them difficult problems, their confidence plummeted and they later lied about their scores."[1]

This insight refers to what is often called "mindset." Dweck's book *Mindset: The New Psychology of Success* is an intriguing read as it explores through many experiments and stories how mindset is developed and changed.[2] Various creative experiments led Dr. Dweck and her colleagues to recognize the importance of developing in young people a "growth mindset" rather than a "fixed mindset." Undoubtedly Professor Miller has some continuing-generation students in her class who have the mindset that intelligence is a fixed quantity and cannot be expanded beyond one's basic intelligence level. These students believe they can succeed in college because they have been told by their parents and others that they have the required amount of intelligence. A corollary of this in their minds is that it would be very risky to take on something that is beyond the usual challenges of college work, because if they come up short, they would call into question their basic and fixed level of intelligence as the basis for future success.[3]

Our careful look at Professor Miller's dialogue with her three students after class has revealed that she probably has several different challenges in addressing the barriers to confidence that inhibit some of her students from achieving their full potential.

STRATEGIES TO BUILD STUDENT CONFIDENCE

What are some useful strategies that professors have developed to build students' self-confidence, whether they are first-generation or continuing-generation students? In the student-based research conducted by Heritage University's Institute for Student Identity and Success to ascertain effective strategies, students identified several of Professor Ernesto "Charro" Cruz's approaches as especially helpful. Professor Cruz, who has developed his strategies over the last ten years, teaches in the Business Major and in Organizational Studies at Heritage University.

Tapping into Prior Expertise

On the first day of class, Professor Cruz talks to the students about what knowledge and background they are bringing to this class. He lists experiences they have had that have taught them some of the basic ideas and principles upon which this class is based, so they are not starting out as entirely ignorant in this field. Since his usual teaching assignments are in the area of organizational development, he can refer to learning that students have already acquired in such matters as how to keep peace in the family, how to help family or friends prepare for big celebrations, how to work in student clubs at school to achieve goals, how to get younger family members to participate successfully in family activities, and related examples. He uses this approach to convince students of two things that will build their confidence. First, they are entering this class with some basic knowledge of this topic; they are not a blank slate. Second, they hold some of the responsibility for this class to fully explore the key topics, and they are expected to share their observations and learnings and/or to ask questions when their experience does not mesh with what they are reading or hearing. Professor Cruz summarizes these important early comments to the class by telling them that he is their coach in this subject, but they are responsible for their own learning.

This same approach can be used on the first day with most classes. It takes a little ingenuity and planning on the part of the professor to carry out this introductory strategy effectively. Wracking your brain for aspects of daily living that can be explained by some of the concepts in the upcoming course, you can surprise and motivate the students by tapping into their practical experiences in a way they have not thought about before. Examining the content in most courses in the humanities, in writing, in most professional fields, and even in many science areas can produce examples that will interest students and build their confidence about being able to succeed in the class.

To address the concern of some first-gen students, mentioned earlier in this chapter, who are afraid of upstaging their parents as they succeed in college courses, the professor can use this same approach of tapping into already-existing expertise that parents of first-gen students may have. At the beginning of the course, the professor probably will not know much about her students nor her students' parents, but the same preparatory brainstorming will usually yield several areas of expertise or practices or skills that can be referenced by asking how many students have parents who can [do something] or who are skilled in [a process or activity]. For instance, in a literature class, she can ask, "How many of you have a parent or aunt or uncle who is a great story-teller?" "Who can tell us about a parent who is a great story-teller?" For a math or science class, questions might refer to some aspect of managing money, or completing house repairs, or dealing with measurements in cooking or sewing. After this conversation with students, the professor can give students a suggestion. "Sometime you could thank your parent(s) for being a role model in demonstrating their expertise to do [such-and-such]. Tell them this motivates you to do well in this class because you are building on what they already gave you through their example." Without mentioning it directly, the professor is subtly building a bridge between key members of the student's non-college-going family and the education he or she is now pursuing. When this happens, students can feel more confident that "I can do it" because they are building on abilities of their own family members.

Sharing Prior Challenges

Often New Majority students have the feeling that they are the only ones experiencing angst and lack of confidence as they pursue their academic work. One way to help students feel that they are not alone in navigating those uncomfortable doubts and anxieties is for the professor to share a personal story of being in a situation where he or she was inexperienced, felt like an outsider, and only gained confidence gradually by working hard at it. If the professor came from a first-gen and/or poverty-level family, he or she is in an ideal position to help students feel they are understood and not alone. However, those professors who do not have this background to share can review other aspects of their lives where their self-confidence was significantly challenged. That might be in some sport in which the professor had very little team experience but lots of interest.[4] Or it might be a story of auditioning for a band or orchestra, passing the audition and being invited to join a well-established group, but lacking self-confidence about how to participate successfully in the band. If the professor does not have a self-confidence story that he or she feels comfortable talking about, there may be a family member, cousin, or friend whose challenge with self-confidence in a specific setting will make a good story to share.

The most important aspect of sharing a personal story about how a significant self-confidence challenge was handled is the enumeration of the steps taken that gradually allowed the person to overcome the anxiety and diffidence. What motivated you to step out of a personal comfort zone and try out the new behavior in spite of not being confident? How did you find allies to help support the new behavior? Undoubtedly there were one or more setbacks on the journey to self-confidence. How did you overcome them? Who insisted that you move forward in spite of your lack of self-confidence? How did you feel about that person at the time? How do you feel about him or her today?

By sharing a personal story and combining it with frequent reassurances to students that they will gain confidence in speaking up, giving oral presentations, asking good questions, and being successful in this subject area, the barrier of poor self-confidence will gradually disappear.

"Bumping into" Students on Campus

One of the most effective ways professors can overcome the self-confidence challenge is something they can do outside class. The diffidence that causes students to hold back from participating in class discussions or asking questions or volunteering to participate in special learning opportunities is often mitigated when they run into their professors in the cafeteria, the library, on the green, or even in the parking lot. Professor Cruz has used this very effectively by regularly dropping into the Heritage University library, the academic skills center, and the dining hall. When he sees one of his students, he approaches and informally greets the student, and asks how everything is going. Students report that this often allows them to ask questions that they didn't have the courage to ask during class. With a little careful observation, professors can generally identify places on campus where they occasionally run into their course participants. That is a clue about where and when it would be most effective to "hang out" on campus periodically, especially early in the course, so that the professor can strike up relaxed, informal interactions that encourage students to ask questions or make comments that they are reticent to do in class. Initially, this may happen with a small group of students from the class, perhaps three to five, and the conversation may all be simply small talk and friendly banter. A student who uses this way of approaching a professor with a question will often hang back as the rest of the student group moves on, and the professor has to be sensitive enough to this subtle move by the student to remain focused and encourage the student to speak his or her mind.

By finding the best places on campus to run into students for informal conversation, especially during the first weeks of the class term, the professor will be building student self-confidence, which can then flower within the classroom and in front of their fellow students.[5]

ADDITIONAL CONSIDERATIONS

It should be noted that there is a body of research around what has been termed "self-efficacy" that relates to but is broader than our topic of student self-confidence. The analysis and strategies proposed in this chapter are intended to address just one aspect of the larger topic of self-efficacy, namely the issue of self-confidence for students who are entering an entirely new realm not previously experienced by their families.[6] Self-efficacy is defined by the American Psychology Association as follows:

Self-efficacy refers to an individual's belief in his or her capacity to execute behaviors necessary to produce specific performance attainments . . . Self-efficacy reflects confidence in the ability to exert control over one's own motivation, behavior, and social environment. These cognitive self-evaluations influence all manner of human experience, including the goals for which people strive, the amount of energy expended toward goal achievement, and likelihood of attaining particular levels of behavioral performance.[7]

In exploring New Majority students' difficulties with self-confidence, we have considered factors related specifically to typical sociocultural differences: those associated with various racial or ethnic cultures and the typical behavior expectations in those cultures, and those associated with living in lower socioeconomic, non-college-going communities. This clarification is important because often students from these backgrounds who are dealing with a lack of self-confidence in the academic setting may actually have strong self-confidence in other settings where their experience and family support have fostered it. It is important that when professors make reference to the self-confidence issues of New Majority students in an academic setting, they do not overgeneralize about a presumed general lack of self-efficacy and self-concept in these students. In other settings, these same individuals may exhibit strong self-confidence and be highly effective.

Think of this point as similar to a situation where a sports coach on an ocean front is introducing surfing to a competent basketball player, coming from a plains state far from the ocean. The player will be suffering from fear of this almost overwhelming new setting with waves crashing onto the sand, and uncertainty about whether the physical skills he has will be sufficient for this new sport. It will make a big difference in how the new surfer feels about this coach, depending on how the coach appears to be seeing him. If the coach treats him as if he is always a hesitant, fearful person and has few physical skills, the new surfer may not learn as readily and will not feel empowered by the coach. But if the coach refers to skills and courage he would have demonstrated as a basketball player, even though the coach did not know him in that setting, this approach will elicit more quickly the new surfer's confidence in the coach and in his own will to try out his surfboard on the waves.

We have reviewed in this chapter various ways to strengthen students' confidence in their ability to succeed in the collegiate world. As you consider the best approaches to use with your students, you will be most effective if you also try to discern the source of the challenges to their confidence that students are experiencing. By being aware that they most likely have confidence and are successful in some other settings that are nonacademic, you will be better equipped to pick strategies appropriate to their needs, and students will be more apt to see you as a welcome ally.

CHAPTER 11

Journaling for Confidence and Deeper Thinking

JASPER AND PERLA were sitting next to each other at two computers at a long study table in the library. They had recently become friends after discovering they had three of their four second-semester classes together. Now they were laboring over an assignment from their Introduction to Statistics class.

Perla looked over at Jasper's fingers lying idly on his keyboard. He was periodically flexing them and looked like he was trying to figure out what to write next. She whispered, "Hey, Jasper. Are you struggling with that journaling assignment? A crazy assignment, if you ask me."

Jasper nodded. "What does this have to do with statistics?" Then he shook his head. He was feeling both a little baffled and quite frustrated. "I really liked the statistics problem, 'cuz it was about our own town. It was pretty interesting. And I think I got all the analysis stuff right. But look at the next part of the assignment!" He pointed to the handout they had received in class yesterday.

As she leaned over to see what Jasper was pointing at, Perla read, "It says, 'Complete your journal entry for this week by writing one of the following two reflections. You can choose either one.'" Perla added in a disgusted tone of voice, "Big deal."

She continued reading: "Number one: 'As you reflect on how you solved this statistics problem, describe ways you could see that this problem-solving process could apply to other situations in your life, especially nonacademic ones.' And number two: 'Describe what specific aspects of this statistics problem were frustrating for you and why, how you dealt with those feelings, and what you learned from this about managing yourself and your frustrations.'" Looking up at Jasper she added, "I just don't understand why we have to do these journal things every week! Why doesn't the professor stick to statistics?"

Jasper murmured, "Maybe Professor Evans didn't have time to create another good statistics problem for us, so he gave us journal questions to keep us busy."

"Well, it just makes me feel like he isn't doing his job as a professor," Perla said. She was talking out loud now. "He's the professor and we're the students. He's supposed to be teaching us what we're supposed to learn, not making us think up things to write down!"

At that moment both Perla and Jasper turned their heads slightly to see one of the library staff walking up behind them. The library assistant whispered, "I know you'd like to share ideas, but remember that we're trying to keep the library a quiet place to study. Could you save your conversation for later, please?"

The two students looked at each other and then looked up sheepishly at the library assistant. "Sorry. Yeah, we'll be quiet," Jasper volunteered. And both of them went back to looking at their keyboards, trying to decide what to write.

WHAT'S GOING ON HERE?

Jasper and Perla are fairly typical of many first-gen students. They come to college with a preconceived notion of what their learning process will be. This is partially based on the teaching-learning settings in their high schools. It is also the result of unconsciously comparing their college setting to the only other outside-the-family adult experience they know, namely a job. Since they are now adults and the adults they know are, mostly, engaged in the job market rather than higher education, they are seeing their entrance into a college experience in much the same way that they see adult employment. Many of them are employed, part-time or full-time, so they have direct experience that forms their views of the "contract" that, tacitly or explicitly, exists between employee and employer. The contract concept goes something like this: you meet the requirements described to you when you were hired—the days, hours, and tasks required in this job—and the employer will pay you. That's the employee's side of the contract. As for the employer, you presume that he or she will not only pay you but also provide what you need to fulfill his or her expectations—uniform, safe working environment, information about the product or service, and the tools and materials required to do the job. That's the basic content of the contract that you as an employee expect from the employer. In addition to the work world, young adults observe the same underlying contract scenario when they open a bank account or receive a driver's license.

It is not surprising, then, that young adult first-gen students automatically apply the same understanding to the unfamiliar environment of the college. Their assumption is that there is a tacit contract they have entered into. "I have paid my tuition and fees and I will read the books assigned and show up at most classes. The professor is responsible to have at his or her fingertips all the knowledge expected in Course X. He or she is responsible to communicate that information to me in a way I can understand and with as much completeness as possible. This is the tacit contract I have entered into between me and my professor by signing up for Course X."

Several academic researchers in Britain have explored this concept of *contract* that many students—typically first-gen students but also some continuing-generation students—have as an unspoken mental picture of their enrollment in higher education.[1] The implication is that if the college or university does not live up to one or more aspects of the implicit contract, then the student has no obligation to feel guilty or to feel like a failure if he or she decides to withdraw. This reality obviously has many repercussions for the way in which every aspect of the university's interaction with students should be handled, from the work of the janitorial staff to the admissions and financial aid offices, to the registrar and course scheduling process, and to many other aspects of college administration. But most clearly, this unspoken assumption about a contractual relationship between the professor and the student can have a significant effect in the classroom. Here's a succinct statement of the problem as explained by Nicholson and colleagues writing in *Studies in Higher Education*: "Some students enter higher education with an unrealistic expectation that they will be provided with all the information they are required to learn . . . and do not expect to have to engage in independent study [and thinking]."[2]

If Perla and Jasper have come to college with this common supposition, even though they have never articulated it, an assignment to do journaling will sound like a useless, "make-work" requirement. Here is another mismatch. From the perspective of these students, the professor is supposed to be teaching the content identified in the course, that is, transferring the course knowledge from the professor's head into theirs. From the perspective of Professor Evans, it is part of his teaching responsibility to help students begin to apply the content of the course to the real world beyond college and to practice the type of independent critical thinking that is needed for lifelong learning. He knows this is essential to building the necessary level of student confidence.

It is remarkable how much effort it takes to convince New Majority students that a crucial part of their college education is personally finding, creating, and assessing knowledge and ideas on their own. Developing one's own ideas is critical to success in academia and in the twenty-first century workforce, and therefore necessary for building one's own self-confidence going forward. In addition, student journals offer faculty a vehicle for sharing comments and building a relationship with students that can also build their confidence as learners.

We already examined one aspect of this challenge in chapter 8 when we explored ways to help students plan ahead for quiet, intense study time. Another piece of this challenge comes to the fore when we look at students' reactions to assignments given by professors to stimulate the students' creative thinking. Journaling is one of these very effective but potentially misunderstood assignments. We have seen from Perla and Jasper's reactions that they have not yet discovered the role of personal, independent analysis and thought as key components of their college education. Consequently, the journaling assignment seems to be sidetracking them from the knowledge transfer that Professor Evans is supposed to be accomplishing for his students.

A recent research-based project verified this misconception about how college learning takes place. Rebecca Cox, author of the insightful book *The College Fear Factor: How Students and Professors Misunderstand One Another*, conducted research by sitting in for a full term on composition classes at community colleges and visiting with the students at different points in the term. One of her findings was illustrated in a particularly blunt way by how students in one class responded to a composition instructor. Professor Cox had observed her developing excellent discussion questions that she gave her students for roundtable or small group work and was impressed by the thoughtfulness and quality of the questions that could lead students to see implications and apply critical reasoning. But when Cox talked to the students after the class, she discovered that they had a totally different interpretation for these discussion activities. They thought the professor had abandoned her responsibility to "inform them" as their instructor and gave them these activities just to save herself from having to teach. They also reported that during the small group discussion times, they began by sharing a few thoughts about the question they were given, but then spent most of the time visiting with each other about personal and social interests, because they didn't see how this activity directly related to the course objectives. The professor had no idea that this was the interpretation students gave her carefully planned group activities. Her preconceived expectation about group discussions and deeper learning was entirely different than that of her students, and she had never explored this candidly with the students.[3] Cox summarizes with this observation: "Many students . . . defined instruction that was not delivered in the form of a lecture as no instruction whatsoever . . . This meant that alternatives to the lecture format tended to be viewed as diversions or a waste of class time."[4]

The conversation between Jasper and Perla about journaling shows this same lack of understanding that students frequently have about non-lecture learning activities. Students are unaware of the variety of effective college-level learning activities that professors can use to help students go deeper into the learning process, and how these activities are legitimate means that professors use to fulfill their responsibilities— their part of the college contract. Another example of misinterpreting professor-required learning activities is the one about small discussion groups detailed by Professor Cox above. In both cases, it is evident that professors of New Majority students always need to precede any learning activities other than lecturing with explicit rationales for the specific activity. If these explanations are not given, students may deliberately withhold their involvement and engagement because they do not think the exercise is an appropriate request from the professor.

Below we will explore one specific, highly effective non-lecturing activity, journaling, and how it can be successfully incorporated into the learning process. But before launching a journaling component in a course, it is important for the professor to explain carefully and fully how this activity is designed to bridge the gap between the abstract information communicated in lectures and assigned reading, and the deepening personal academic lives of the students as they move toward becoming professionals in their chosen field.

STRATEGIES FOR EFFECTIVE JOURNALING

There are several reasons that professors might choose to incorporate journaling assignments into courses. From the journaling questions that Perla and Jasper have before them, it appears that Professor Evans has two primary purposes in mind: 1) getting students to reflect on the process they used to accomplish an assignment, thereby moving them toward a more robust understanding of an important concept or skill; and 2) helping students make a connection between their academic work and their personal or family lives in order to help them see they are benefiting right now from their educational experience, and not only after they complete their degree and enter their chosen field of work. Both of these are very worthwhile goals, but the reaction that Perla and Jasper had regarding their journaling assignment demonstrates why this exercise is especially useful with New Majority students. The students' incorrect assumption that all knowledge and learning will be presented directly by their professor can be gradually replaced through journaling exercises by academia's premise that students must discover much of their learning through their own work individually and in collaboration with other students, in order to acquire the critical thinking skills and confidence in one's own ideas that are vital for life-long learning.

An additional outcome that professors need to achieve with many New Majority students as well as some diffident continuing-gen students is making a connection with each student so each feels personally supported by the professor and therefore personally responsible to respond to the professor's high expectations. By writing comments on students' journal entries, professors have an opportunity to make the personal connections that may be hard to make outside of class because most New Majority students tend not to linger on campus due to their job and family responsibilities.

Journal entries can be assigned through the syllabus at regular intervals throughout the course, such as weekly, or after the completion of each major unit. Professors can also use the last ten minutes of each class for students to start writing a journal entry, which assures that they begin to think about the topic for a specific journal entry. Normally they would complete the entry as they do their homework follow-up for that class session. But even if they don't do their homework, by giving them ten minutes at the end of class, they have begun to turn the question over in their minds. This may be a subtle but effective way to begin involving students who have not yet engaged in the course.

At Heritage University, Professor Sara Cartmel experimented with various ways of employing journaling. Her goals were to encourage students to engage in deeper thinking and to apply their course work learning to their own lives. Over several years and many experiments, she developed an approach that we identified through our research with undergraduates as very effective.[5] To be successful at increasing New Majority students' confidence and leading them to deeper thinking, we observed that the following strategies work well.

Give Specific Writing Prompts

Just asking students to "keep a journal about this class" without more explicit guidelines is not usually helpful, especially for first-gen students. But giving them specific writing prompts each time a journal entry is required has the potential of leading students to deeper thinking and connecting them with the professor. As the professor develops the writing prompt for a specific class session or assignment, the following touchstones provide helpful ways to evaluate whether it will be effective with students:

- The writing prompt relates to the course content
- The writing prompt provides a clear focus for the student's writing
- The writing prompt is open-ended enough to allow the student several avenues of response
- The writing prompt asks the student to reflect on a concept or to apply the concept

Developing good journaling prompts requires practice, and Professor Cartmel provides some helpful suggestions about how to start a prompt:

- *Think about . . .*
- *Identify . . .*
- *What may have caused . . .*
- *What effects will result from . . .*
- *Explore how you could . . .*
- *Write about choices you could make to . . .*
- *How will you apply this concept . . .*

Establish Guidelines for Journal Entries

When a professor introduces students to the role of journaling in the class, there are several factors to consider. It is helpful to find out initially if students have experienced journaling assignments in previous classes. If so, discovering exactly how journaling was handled in the earlier courses is important, because you may wish to make clear how your process matches or differs from the students' earlier experiences. For instance, students may have been told to write journal entries in class, but the professor does not read them and instead walks up and down the aisles glancing over each student's open journal to verify that each is actually writing something. This model is not what is described here, and students need to know that from the beginning.

Once you know what earlier experiences of journaling, if any, they have had, you can share the guidelines you will be using as you read their journals and make comments on them. The three most important criteria (or rubrics, if this terminology is familiar to these students) that Professor Cartmel uses to evaluate student journal entries are *Honesty*, *Thoroughness*, and *Depth*. It is helpful to share a short definition of each of these, or other criteria that you may choose. Better yet, share examples that demonstrate these criteria. By specifying *Honesty* Professor Cartmel intends to make it clear that students can say whatever they are feeling or thinking, even if they believe it is not what the professor thinks. She also uses this criterion in hopes that it will create a feeling of openness and lack of fear within students so they can get in touch with their real feelings and thoughts. The criterion of *Thoroughness* is meant to encourage more robust journal entries. Many professors at Heritage have shared with me their frustration early in their courses when students give extremely short answers to questions, both orally and in writing. By asking for thoroughness the student is encouraged to elaborate on the basic idea that he or she first writes, explaining in more detail an initial short thought so that the full meaning is evident. The conventional questions of "who," "what," and "when" may help stimulate more thoroughness. The criterion of *Depth* is perhaps the most difficult one to identify in specific journal entries, but Professor Cartmel tries to help students by specifying that they should ask themselves "why" and "how" after every sentence as they write their entries. After a thought is initially written down, if the student asks herself "Why do I think that?" or "How is this actually true?" he or she will usually find an additional depth of understanding to add to the journal entry. Another question could be "What else is related to this?" Depending upon the subject matter of the course, a professor may be able to pose additional helps for students to achieve greater depth in their journal entries.

A difficult concept for some first-gen students to grasp in their first college classes is that there are no "wrong answers" in a journaling entry. And yet there are journal entries that do not meet one of the three criteria and consequently are not going to get the full points available for a fully satisfactory entry. If students are familiar with the personal practice of keeping a diary, it will be easier to explain this point. The significance of clarifying the "no wrong answers" instruction is that students need to feel free to write whatever they honestly think in relation to the writing prompt, without worrying that they will get "points taken off" if they state something from the current course topic that is incorrect. This leaves them free to state misconceptions or confusions about the topic and therefore gives the professor a chance to clarify, either through comments written on the journal entry or if it appears to be an important clarification for everyone, with the whole class at the next session.

At the same time that the professor makes clear the "no wrong answers in a journal entry" standard, a discussion with the class about the three criteria is appropriate. This may occur before they write their first journal entries, or later when there are practical examples to demonstrate what "thoroughness" or "depth" mean in this context.

Comments That Promote Confidence

Journaling is most effective when the professor takes the time, at least periodically, to read the journal entries and write comments on them. To help build student confidence, professors can write comments that point out especially insightful self-awareness in an entry. Even short comments written on the paper, such as "Outstanding insight" or "Excellent depth" or more informal comments that help build a connection with the student, such as "Awesome" or "Wow" will help build student confidence.[6]

Somewhat longer comments—a sentence or two—are very helpful in encouraging both greater self-awareness and deeper thinking. Some students will be coming out of a cultural setting (ethnic or socioeconomic or gender) where expressing one's personal reflective feelings is normally not acceptable. For these students, encouragement from the professor to reflect seriously on "how I am feeling about this learning process" is essential if the students are to take full ownership for their learning in college. In addition to encouraging comments on the journal entry, a professor can write a follow-up question, sparking further reflection and thinking by the student.

Another effective type of comment is the one that recognizes evidence of deeper thinking by the student. Since many New Majority students don't really believe that, at this stage of their maturity and education, they can have any significant ideas beyond those they are memorizing or learning from the professor and the textbook, any sign of an original idea from them should receive a special comment from the professor. By encouraging such preliminary steps into *deep thinking*, a professor may become a crucial bridge, helping build the crossover from the rote learning presumptions of many first-gen students into the realization that higher education is only truly effective when it includes their unique contributions of analysis and applying new ideas to study and life.

SUMMARY

Incorporating journaling into any course, when it is done thoughtfully and carefully, can be an effective strategy for helping New Majority students increase their confidence and discover that they can explore new ideas at a level they never knew was possible. It can also be a way in which students begin to feel a personal connection with their professor, especially in a larger class where it is difficult for professors to interact face-to-face with all students. Based on the family cultures of many New Majority students, feeling a personal connection with a professor is more important than is usually recognized. A recent dissertation research project conducted by Ricardo Valdez with students in a university that is majority first-generation uncovered the finding that when these students experience personal interest from a professor, they identify this as a major factor in achieving subsequent success.[7] In terms of the interdependence value we discussed earlier, meeting the caring expectations of someone you look up to is indeed a very high priority. One first-gen student interviewed in the research expressed this clearly when he talked about two or three professors who had given him personal encouragement: "I want to do well *for them*, because I am given a lot of responsibility and it is *also very important for them that I do well*" (emphasis added).[8] Another student said about his professor, *"He believes in me and I don't want to let him down"* (emphasis added).[9]

Professors can use journaling as a regular course practice, making individualized comments on journal entries that will build students' confidence, motivation, and commitment to becoming wholeheartedly engaged in their college education.

CHAPTER 12

Developing Students' Own Academic Ideas

MY RESEARCH ASSISTANT, Tina, was almost twenty minutes late, which wasn't like her. When she arrived breathless at my office door, the explanation tumbled out of her.

"My friend, Kayla—she was crying and I had to stay with her till she was better."

I responded sympathetically. "Of course you did. What happened to Kayla?"

"She's been having an awful time in her sociology class. That prof is really picky. He told them to write a paper on some sociology topic—I didn't get what it was—but the assignment was to write their own ideas about it. Kayla got her first paper handed back to her with 'Not accepted' written at the top and a note that it didn't contain any of her own ideas."

"So did she write it again with her own opinions?" I asked.

"She told me she went back to the readings they had on that topic and she carefully picked out a different set of ideas than in her first paper. She kept saying, 'I picked everything I said on my own, and I rewrote the ideas in my own words.' That's how she prepared the revision for her professor. She really thought she was meeting his requirement to 'write your own ideas' *because she worked hard to put the ideas she found into her own words. But she got the second paper back with the same notes on it! Her second paper said again, 'Need to write your own ideas.' She swears that she didn't copy anyone else's paper, and she is really frustrated."*

I was beginning to see another typical communication mismatch with first-gen students surfacing. "I'm sure she didn't copy anyone else's paper," I said. "But it sounds like she was rewriting the ideas from the readings and not really giving her own, original ideas. Do you think she really understood what the professor meant by 'her own ideas'?"

Tina grimaced. "Yeah. You're right. I don't think she really knew what that assignment meant. I told her she should think up some new ideas that weren't in the readings, things that no way were in what she already read. I said that's what the professor probably meant by 'your own ideas.'"

"Well, you were right on, Tina," I responded. "Did that help Kayla see what she has to do?"

"Not really. Kayla said she might have a few ideas of her own, but she didn't think they were really worth sharing, and she was very scared to try to write them so the professor would like them. And besides, she said, 'Why would the professor want to hear any of my ideas? I'm only a sophomore and this is my first sociology class!' I didn't know what to tell her. But I remembered struggling with that different kind of thinking from the professor in my first English class, so I told her she should go to the Writing Center. That's where they helped me. Maybe they can help her."

"Excellent advice, Tina. I think they will," I responded.

WHAT'S GOING ON HERE?

As I reflected back on my conversation with Tina, I concluded, "It's certainly not rocket science to figure out what the problem was with Tina's friend." Obviously Kayla did not picture the task of finding her own, original thoughts on a subject as a predictable college assignment. She apparently didn't anticipate that she would have to develop her own ideas on the subjects she was studying. And furthermore, she did not believe that she would have any *legitimate* original ideas to write for her professor, even though she might be able to surface some tentative ones. We explored a similar mindset held by many New Majority students in the previous chapter when we talked about the potential for journaling as a way to begin developing students' confidence in their own opinions and encouraging them to reflect on their own experiences and reactions to the course content. But the problem of getting students to surface their own *academic* ideas in relation to a specific assigned topic and then write about it is more difficult. With journaling, because it relates closely to the commonly recognized practice of keeping a diary, students can usually picture writing something from their own personal experience. Students also realize that their journaling will not be judged in the same way as a formal paper focusing on an academic concept. In the case of such a prescribed writing assignment as Kayla had received, there are additional subliminal and internal barriers keeping a New Majority student from believing that her own interpretation and views are worth writing and that they would be accepted by her professor.

In listening to Tina, it became obvious to me that when Kayla was told to "express her own ideas" she interpreted that to mean that she should put the concepts currently under study in "her own words." That may well have been acceptable in her high school classes. Perhaps in earlier college classes, if she was asked to "include her own ideas," she answered by restating the academic thoughts in her own formulation, and the professor grading her paper may have concluded that she wasn't terribly smart and probably didn't have any interesting new ideas to share. In fact, many professors are not aware of the mindset that may prevent even a bright New Majority student from expressing any original ideas.

It is very helpful to professors of New Majority students to understand the background and rationale that influence the mindset of students like Kayla regarding the expression of individual, original thoughts. There is often a mismatch between the professor's expectation that students will *appreciate* the opportunity to express their own original thoughts or write up their own individual view on a topic, and what students are actually thinking. For some minority cultures and some working-class environments, there is a communication norm that strongly discourages the expression of individual and original ideas, especially from young people. This may be due to the importance placed on the pervasive values of community and interdependence within the student's home environment, which we explored in chapter 9. If these have been operative principles in Kayla's life thus far, not only would it have been hard for her to ignore that behavior standard when she started to work on the sociology assignment, but she also would have had the added challenge of beginning something that she has had very little practice doing.[1]

Once she understood what the professor really wanted, and once she could overcome her initial inclination to avoid expressing her unique ideas, exploring the assigned concept within her own mind, on her own and not with others, would require her to formulate new associations, new implications, and new comparisons that could then constitute the original ideas the professor had requested. That would be quite a task! Students experiencing this kind of challenge often need additional assistance to gain the experience and confidence necessary to become proficient at discovering and then expressing their own ideas. The strategy section, below, shares some ways to achieve this.

Some first-gen students have been independent thinkers from childhood, even though they may have expressed those original thoughts only rarely. But as they enter college, they may be inhibited from expressing their own ideas because they lack the cultural capital that comes from traveling in circles with college-educated parents or friends.[2] Another way to say this is that they have observed interactions among their middle-class student peers and professors in which both body language and speech characteristics are different than those that are typical within their own home environments. This disconnect automatically produces a hesitancy and insecurity that causes first-gen students to be afraid to share their own thoughts or to ask for help. It directly affects their reticence about engaging in oral conversations with professors and more experienced classmates. But it also affects their concerns about writing papers, because they are afraid that the language they use in their writing will reflect how they speak, and they often have memories of when they or their New Majority classmates received unexpected negative reactions to their oral comments or story-telling because of vocabulary, grammar, slang, or even body language that reflected a different sociocultural world. Encounters like that reinforce the first-gen students' determination to be very cautious about when and how they express themselves. Having observed these subtle but real differences in communication norms from their first days on campus, they are naturally reticent to lay themselves open to similar criticism or even to ridicule. Applying this reality to Kayla's case, we can guess that even if she understands more correctly what the professor means by "your own ideas," she will want to hold back in stating those ideas for fear of not using acceptable language and, if she is asked to share orally, of not demonstrating appropriate nonverbal behavior.

A third source of reticence about expressing one's original ideas could be attributed to stereotype threat experienced by a student whose ethnicity or socioeconomic class or gender or sexual orientation or age is obviously not the norm in a given collegiate setting. As we have seen in an earlier discussion on stereotype threat in chapter 4, becoming aware that there could be negative connotations to one or more aspects of your identity will trigger in you a stress reaction that has been consistently measured in brain research. This stress reaction interferes with your deeper thinking processes, making what you express less robust and/or proficient than it would have been without the stress reaction.[3]

Now that we understand the one or more reasons why Kayla and other New Majority students may not be prepared to identify or express their own ideas on an academic topic, it is helpful to note the findings that University of Texas at San Antonio Professor Laura Rendón's research has produced, referred to as "validation theory." Her work with Latino students at four-year colleges to identify what made them successful led to the somewhat unexpected primary conclusion that the most important factor was having someone who *validated* them: "Validating agents took an active interest in students. They provided encouragement for students and affirmed them as being capable of academic work and supported them in their academic endeavors and social adjustment."[4] The important insight is that it took just one person who actively validated a New Majority student to create a significant change toward success for the student. With someone who validated a learner with the message "You can do it," the student grew from a state of lacking the confidence to try new skills—such as thinking through and expressing original ideas—into becoming a successful student who would explore and adopt many of the new skills a successful college student needs.[5]

STRATEGIES TO HELP STUDENTS SURFACE THEIR OWN IDEAS

Most experienced English professors have developed some unique ways of getting reticent students to explore and express their own ideas. They may not know, however, how the lack of confidence sparked by stereotype threat and different sociocultural norms can complicate this task. Often they are baffled as to why students are so shy about expressing their own ideas, or seemingly so unskilled at this apparently straightforward task. The evidence that New Majority students are especially likely to fall into this group has been documented in various recent research projects, such as the one conducted by Krista Soria and Michael Stebleton of the University of Minnesota Twin Cities. Based on a survey of almost two thousand first-year students at a large university, they found a statistically significantly lower rate for first-gen students, in comparison with continuing-gen students, of contributing to class discussions, bringing up ideas from other courses, or asking insightful questions during class. Lower levels of all these behaviors are consistent with not writing one's own ideas in a requested paper. This research should give new energy and motivation to professors who already have strategies for getting students to surface and write about their own ideas, as well as generating interest in finding new strategies. The important new insight is this: for many New Majority students, what is holding them back is not laziness or a lack of intelligence, but a combination of factors in their social and cultural milieu for which they are not responsible. They deserve all the help we can give them. The creative and insightful ideas that these inexperienced students frequently produce once they overcome their lack of confidence makes it all worthwhile. In this section, we will explore the creative solutions that two professors who were identified in our student research are using.

Schedule Several "Seminar Days"

We have noted earlier that appealing to New Majority students' higher comfort level with interdependence and ensuring their participation in community are effective ways to spark their interest and maintain their motivation. Professor Tom Mount at Yakima Valley Community College (YVCC) pairs this insight with an emphasis on getting students to express personal opinions about academic topics in a format he refers to as "the seminar." He designates several specific class dates during the term as "seminar days," and explains the format and grading system for these ahead of time. He also establishes from the first day of the term that each student has a unique and important role in the class by asking all students to fill out an index card with the name that they would prefer to be called in class, along with their official college-registered name. He draws cards randomly from this stack of name cards whenever he wants to involve students in discussions or get them to comment on assigned readings.

One week in advance of a seminar day, he assigns a reading that will be the subject of the seminar, and includes questions each student must answer in a paper of at least three hundred words and bring to the seminar. The questions are designed to make students pick up the core ideas in the reading and also to elicit their own reactions and ideas. When students arrive at class on the seminar day, they have had time to develop their own thoughts about the topic through their reading and answering the accompanying questions.

QUESTION-STARTERS ON ASSIGNED READING

- *Which idea in this reading was the most interesting to you? Why?*
- *Which idea or information in the article did you already know, and where did you learn this?*
- *Which point in the reading was the hardest to understand? If there is still something confusing to you, please describe it.*
- *If you had to edit the reading to make it shorter, which pages or paragraphs would you cut out?*

■ *If you could ask the author of this reading to write a follow-up article, what would it be about?*

■ *Think of another class you have taken where this article might be appropriate for the teacher to assign and explain why.*

■ *Try to summarize this article in 25 words or less. When you have done this, describe whether this was easy or hard and why.*

Using the index cards, Professor Mount randomly chooses nine to twelve names and those students form the core circle. Students know that everyone's name will be picked at least once for a seminar during the term, but they don't know on which day. As their names are called, core circle students move the desks so that they are sitting in a circle in the center of the room, surrounded on the outside of the circle by all the other students in the class. Then the core circle students begin discussing the assigned reading. The professor has explained to the students in advance that no one is the leader in the circle; they are all equal participants and equally responsible for their seminar session's success. He has also clarified how he will be grading them during their seminar discussion. They earn basic points for being present on the day their name is picked, more points by being a good listener and providing encouragement to their seminar circle peers, and even more points for referencing a specific point in the reading as they express their ideas. Professor Mount, once he has taught this format to students, does not intervene in the discussion, which continues for most of the remaining class time. But he does periodically interrupt to draw the name of someone in the outer circle and asks him or her to paraphrase what a circle participant has just said. Correctly stating what has been said earns points for that student in the outer circle. This process keeps the entire class on their toes, because no one knows when the professor will interrupt and call on one of the observers to paraphrase what a core circle member has just said. It also encourages the circle members to speak loudly enough to be heard throughout the room and motivates them to share their ideas with enough clarity that paraphrasing by an outer circle student is possible.

At the conclusion of a seminar day, all students in attendance have experienced what it means to explore in more depth the ideas contained in course readings. They have personally seen what is meant when a professor requests that they "write their own ideas" in an assignment or project paper. How do we know this? The evidence gathered from YVCC student focus groups helped us to identify Professor Mount's seminar strategy as an effective approach. When sophomores at YVCC were asked to identify specific classroom approaches that were most responsible for their becoming successful, committed students, the seminar strategy was strongly endorsed. Professor Mount also reported that after he started using this strategy a few years ago, he saw a major improvement in students being able to discuss ideas in more depth and to personally engage with content in the course.[6]

Having observed the process in action, I noted three key components. Professors could reconfigure these basic elements in ways that suit their courses and teaching style. To assure that the seminar strategy actually helps students increase their ability to engage topics more deeply and share their own thinking, these components must be included:

- Structuring the seminar sessions so every student in the class is motivated to study in advance the topic or reading and prepare something in writing expressing the student's thoughts.
- Not identifying those who must participate in the core circle on a given day until the scheduled class time; if students knew they would be participating they might be tempted, before the class, to gather ideas *not* their own from those they consider "smarter" than they, before the class.
- Awarding points or grades during the seminar sessions on the basis of evidence that students are really engaged with the subject. The evidence can be judged by observing one of these student behaviors: paraphrasing what someone in the core circle has said; asking a fellow circle participant follow-up questions to his or her comments that lead to greater depth in the discussion; or sharing a thought that specifically references something in the reading and adds a comment about it.

By building on the priority New Majority students place on being part of a community and helping that community succeed, the seminar strategy can motivate students to acquire a skill they may have been resisting: speaking up to express their own ideas in an academic setting.

Brainstorming in Small Groups with a Recorder

This is a different strategy that refers specifically to helping students find their own voice and express their own ideas in written assignments. The strategy starts by having the professor meet with a small group of two to four students for a session that may last anywhere from ten to thirty minutes. It could be done several times during the term, each time with a different group of students, so that all students who are having trouble writing their own ideas can experience this strategy sometime during the term. As you will see, the effectiveness of the strategy becomes evident to students once they experience it. As a follow-up they can utilize the strategy on their own the next time they need it.

Professor Paula Collucci at Heritage University invented this approach, using her cell phone. As the director of the university's writing center, she was looking for a way to be more effective with students who came to the center with this typical request: "I have to write a paper with my own ideas on this topic. I don't have any ideas and I don't know where to start." As a professor who relates very well to students, she knew that she could get them to start talking about an idea if she created an informal setting and posed a series of simple questions.

QUESTION-STARTERS TO SURFACE IDEAS FOR A PAPER

- *What's the topic? Where have you heard of or read of this topic before?*
- *What does this topic remind you of?*
- *What scares you about trying to talk about it?*
- *Who have you heard talking about this already? What did they say?*
- *If you were to hold a town hall meeting about this topic, who should be invited? What would they be advocating for?*
- *If you had to describe this topic to your mom (or younger brother or . . .), what would you say?*
- *Who do you think would really have a lot to say on this topic? Why?*

She then listened intently to responses, using follow-up questions. She saw that it would begin to dawn on students partway through these informal conversations that their own ideas were emerging. She calls this moment with students "entering the conversation." She recalls some students saying with surprise in their voices, "I'm actually sharing my own individual ideas!" and she noted they would then try to jot down some notes. But this usually created an awkward silence as the student was writing and the flow of ideas stopped. One day while she was working with students, she noticed her cell phone sitting on the desk and thought, "Wait a minute. I can record this conversation and send it to the students! Then they won't have to interrupt their thought flow by trying to take notes."

She moved the phone to the center of the small round table where two students were sitting with her, shared her idea with them, asked them to put down their pens, got their okay to turn on the recording app on her phone, and continued encouraging the conversation with her questions and genuine interest. When she was satisfied that each of the students had indeed expressed some solid, interesting, personal ideas about the topic, she turned off the recording mechanism and told the students, "Watch your e-mail later today. I will be e-mailing you this recording. If you have a smartphone, you can listen to it from your phone. If not, you can use your computer or one of the student computers on campus to bring up your e-mail. Look for the one from me, click on the attachment, and you'll hear yourselves talking. You will be surprised how many of your own ideas surfaced during our conversation here! Listen carefully to yourselves and take notes, just the way you do during a professor's lecture in class. Then use those notes to write your paper. You will have your own ideas to form the basis for your paper!"

This inventive approach to helping students, by having them hear their own recorded ideas, was a hit from the first time Professor Collucci used it.[7] As she continued to employ this method, she noticed that frequently students would totally forget that they were being recorded once the conversation got under way. Often students would return to the writing center after they received her e-mail with the attached recording to say excitedly, "I just couldn't believe that I had all those ideas!" Once students had participated successfully in one of these brainstorming sessions with Professor Collucci and heard themselves saying ideas that were their very own, she encouraged them to use the same technique by themselves or with a couple of other students. Some had phones that could record and send the conversation as an e-mail attachment, just as the professor's did, and by sharing their phones with other students, they could all listen to themselves, take notes, and have the necessary content for writing their papers.

Professor Collucci follows up the first session where ideas were recorded with the invitation for students to bring back their first draft after they listen to the recording and take notes from it. She has observed that many more students now follow up by returning for a second session than formerly, because of the success they experienced in the first (recording) session. During the second session the topic of structure in the paper can be explored. Additional sessions may then occur because the student is experiencing affirming feedback and support throughout the difficult challenge of writing a paper that reflects the student's personal analysis of information, as well as correct mechanics.

SUMMARY

It is of vital importance that professors of New Majority students find ways to help them identify and develop their ability to think deeply about subjects and generate their own observations, opinions, and insights. Until they have gained confidence that they can do this and that the rest of society wants to hear what they have to say, they are unlikely to persevere to graduation. This is a tragedy. Their communities need their contributions and leadership. We all need their contributions and leadership. We will not benefit from their hidden talents unless we help them unlock that inner door that prevents them from believing in themselves, their ability to think and analyze on their own, and therefore their ability to make a difference in the world.

STRATEGIES TO BUILD A VISION FOR THE FUTURE

AS STUDENTS advance into courses that are central to their major and related directly to their future careers, the work generally gets a bit tougher. What often keeps students going and motivates them to work harder than they have ever worked before is the connection they see between these advanced concepts or challenging assignments and their future career. But if this connection is vague or unclear, New Majority students may find it harder to persevere and maintain the confidence to be dedicated to more difficult academic work.

In recent years, many academic programs have now begun to include "high-impact practices" that have been identified through extensive research as beneficial to student learning.[1] They include three that can relate directly to helping New Majority students envision their futures: undergraduate research opportunities, community-based or service learning, and internships.[2] These effective approaches support students' efforts to envision their futures, and they are usually adopted because each can be tied directly to a specific discipline and/or profession. Professors will have a significant positive impact on New Majority students as they find ways to incorporate one or more of these opportunities in any course that is directly pointed toward a given profession. Strategies in the next section illustrate how faculty can help students prepare for these opportunities by envisioning an academic identity as well as developing a practical and realistic vision of themselves in a professional setting.

CHAPTER 13

Envisioning an Academic Identity

How Professors Can Help

SOME YEARS AGO, a young woman named Martha drove into the campus in the middle of the morning and hesitantly walked into the building closest to the parking lot. The first person she met was an administrative assistant who happened to be walking down the hall. Everyone else was busy in class, as it was almost the end of the term.

Martha shyly inquired, "Is there an office where I can learn something about this college?"

The staff member responded cordially, "Follow me. I'll take you to the admissions office." Soon they had walked through the building and across open grass to the small unit where she turned Martha over to the admissions person who was on campus that day, Roy.

Roy welcomed Martha to his office and as he offered her a chair he said, "Thanks for coming in. Hope I can help you. Do you live near the campus?"

Martha looked very reserved but she answered his question readily. "I live just a couple of miles away. I just finished the grocery shopping for my family and was driving home. I usually come this way, and I've been wondering what kind of classes you have and who goes here, so today I thought I'd stop by and see what's going on."

With this opening, Roy took advantage of his visitor's interest to launch into an overview of all the programs and degrees available. As he watched her reactions, he guessed she was probably about twenty-five. She seemed quite interested in everything he shared. He decided to engage her by asking, "So, have you attended college before?"

"Oh no," Martha said. "I did graduate from the high school in town, but my father-in-law says now that I have two kids, my job is to be a good mother and stay at home. We live with him and my mother-in-law, so I couldn't possibly sign up for college."

"But would you like to, if you could?" Roy persisted.

Martha looked at the floor and spoke softly. "Well, maybe. I'd really like to learn something new. I've been thinking about computers. The idea of what they do just blows my mind. It would be fun to learn more about them. And I was thinking, maybe someday when the kids are in school, I could work in an office a few hours a day, if I knew how to use a computer. But I shouldn't be thinking that way. I really can't do that." Her voice trailed off.

Roy was trying to understand her situation a little better. "How come you stopped by our office today?"

"My grocery shopping went pretty fast today. I go to the store almost every day and I'm not expected to be at home for an hour or two, so I thought I could take a few minutes to stop by, and here I am." Martha's explanation ended with a slight smile and Roy began to feel her trust building.

"Well, what if you just took one class that was in the mornings and you planned your shopping around that?" Roy hoped he wasn't pushing too hard. Martha immediately looked interested.

"Maybe I could do that," she said. "I usually have to do other things in town, like gassing up the car, picking up mail at the post office, maybe going to the bakery, things like that. So if I planned really well, maybe I could come for a class." Martha sounded excited, but then her face changed to a crestfallen, almost dejected look. "I don't have any money for classes, though, and I can't ask my family for any," she said quietly.

Roy began telling her about financial aid and led her to the offices down the hall where he introduced her to a financial aid officer. Staying with her as the financial aid discussion unfolded, Roy soon learned that Martha would qualify for both state and federal aid, based on the lack of regular employment for any member of the household. The only sources of household income that Martha could identify in response to the financial aid officer's questions were her husband's and father-in-law's periodic part-time work stints and their catching a few large salmon and selling them several times a year. Roy restated for Martha what the financial aid officer had said: "Martha, if you fill out these forms we'll help you with, you won't have to pay anything to take a class."

Martha was dumbfounded. "Really? Are you sure?" she said. "Well, can I look at the list of classes you showed me in your office?"

Roy reached over and picked up the course schedule for the upcoming term from the financial aid officer's desk. "Here it is. Look, here's an Introduction to Computers class that's offered three days a week from 10:00 to 11:00 a.m. Do you think you could come to that class?"

By this time Martha was getting excited. "Monday, Wednesday, Thursday mornings. And I would be home a little after eleven. I bet I could do that, and they wouldn't miss me at home. I think I could do that. Maybe I won't tell my father-in-law yet. I really don't want to make him mad."

Within another half hour Martha had filled out all the paperwork needed, signed up for Introduction to Computers, been shown the classroom where she needed to show up, and purchased the textbook in the bookstore with a financial aid voucher. About an hour after she had entered the campus, she was back in her car, driving on past the college to her rural residence, and arriving about the same time as she usually did after her daily shopping expeditions.

Roy felt it was important to give a "head's up" to the professor who would be teaching Martha, as it seemed a bit unusual to have a commuter student with kids who might not be letting all of those she lived with know that she was attending college. He made it a point to drop by the professor's office and share basic information about Martha. As the new term started, Roy checked in again with the professor and learned that Martha was coming to class regularly and seemed to be doing well. The professor said that he let her know he was aware of her situation with her family, and had asked her how it was going.

"I haven't felt free yet to tell my father-in-law what I'm doing," she had responded. "Maybe I'll get up my courage soon." Her professor admitted this response left him a bit mystified but that he followed up by asking how she was getting her homework done. (This was an earlier time in the development *of computer technology, so homework meant primarily reading her text.) The professor shared with Roy that Martha said she kept the textbook in her car, and on the days when she didn't come to class, she sat in the parking lot at the grocery store and studied the textbook. Roy just shook his head in amazement. But he felt very good that he had opened a new door for Martha.*

WHAT'S GOING ON HERE?

This story is quite remarkable, and I had a chance to interact with this amazing young woman, Martha, the following semester when she signed up for a class I was teaching during her second term at Heritage University. She shared with me that she had finally confided to her mother-in-law that she was attending class. Her mother-in-law gave Martha a supportive response but told her not to tell her father-in-law, at least not yet. Martha had also let her husband know about attending Heritage and was thrilled when he told her how proud he was of her. He said he admired her bravery in doing what she thought would be good for all of them in the long run, even if the head of the household probably wouldn't agree.

It was fortuitous she was in my class, because I could regularly give her my support. She came for the course faithfully and completed all the assignments. I watched carefully how she fit in with the rest of the class and was amazed that although she remained fairly shy with other students, she appeared to feel she belonged. As I thought about it, and reflected on experiences I had had with other students, it impressed me that she had figured out how to successfully manage two very different identities. This was obviously playing a crucial role in her ability to persevere toward completing an academic program. At Heritage University, she had taken on an academic identity, but in her multigenerational household she was maintaining a family identity, which in public did not include attending any higher education. She regularly shared stories with me about her young boys or other family incidents which indicated that she was fully involved with the family and got along with all of them, including her father-in-law. I was truly impressed, and I learned some important insights from her.

Martha's ability to take on an academic identity while maintaining her family and ethnic cultural identities was in stark contrast to the experience I had had with many other students. They had expressed doubts about whether they could fit into the university milieu, largely because they were concerned about cutting themselves off from their families. What I was learning from Martha was a recognition that it is indeed possible to adopt another identity, become comfortable with and successful in it, and still be able to return to one's older identity or identities and maintain them intact. Furthermore, taking on an academic identity is necessary for envisioning oneself into the future as a college graduate.

STRATEGIES TO HELP STUDENTS ADOPT AN ACADEMIC IDENTITY

From my observations, one of the biggest challenges to New Majority students' perseverance and motivation that will sustain them all the way to graduation is a fear of losing their identity as a respected member of their family, their neighborhood, their ethnic or national group, and their working-class environment. When they initially become involved in higher education, they usually can describe their future career hopes clearly, such as becoming a doctor, a teacher, a lawyer, or other professional. But at that point they are probably unaware that this future job status may also imply a change in their social class. Then, as they begin to observe in their new academic environment the language usage and behavioral interactions among faculty and administrators, their continuing-generation student peers, and professionals in the career they are seeking, the contrast with the behaviors and language used in their home grows more obvious. Naturally their initial reaction in academia is to feel uncomfortable and even incompetent. As this awareness dawns more strongly on New Majority students, no one explains to them the possibility of *assuming an additional identity*. Without familiarity with this concept, their initial reaction to their discomfort in collegiate settings is often "I don't belong here" or "I'm going to lose who I am if I start to behave like these people." This is where the attrition of first-gen students often starts.[1]

Talk About It!

An important step a professor needs to take when trying to motivate New Majority students to continue or deepen their commitment to being successful in their college degree goals is simply to talk about *academic identity* in relation to other identities that the students may have. The reality is that without recognizing or naming it, students have already adopted additional identities as the adults in their lives have instructed them to behave differently in various settings. For instance, they have learned to behave differently in church or at the doctor's office. The example I use when my college students are skeptical of my statement that they already know how to shift identities is this: "Imagine you are back in high school, and with a couple of your buddies you are hanging out at your house. You go into the kitchen to raid the refrigerator for some soft drinks, and you are kidding each other back and forth. Suddenly your grandmother enters the room. Do you start using language differently? Do you change how you are standing or sitting, or how you are interacting with each other?" At this point, the students usually begin to smile and often giggle or smirk as they remember the quick changes they made when a grandparent or other authority figure entered the room.

Many students may not have thought about the concept of *identity*, so you may need to give various examples to help them recognize their own identity shifts that have already taken place. Two basic concepts are key here. One is the idea that the language and behavior a person uses to be accepted in a particular type of setting constitutes most of what we are calling identity. The second equally important idea here is that when a person adopts a new identity to fit into a new setting, it does not require you to abandon who you are as a person—your core identity. The competent adult is able to take on various identities as needed in order to operate effectively in each different environment. As Jane Tapp, professor at the University of Nottingham, United Kingdom, writes: "Despite the potential for conflict, different aspects of identity are not necessarily related in predictable ways; working-class students can create complex identities, in which working-class and academic identities co-exist, and a changing learner identity need not implies [sic] a changing class identity."[2]

Some people refer to this as *contextual shifting*.[3] If students are more comfortable talking about "contextually shifting my identity" than about "shifting my identity" or "adopting an academic identity," professors can be flexible with the terminology.

Use Metaphors

As students adapt to college life by adopting changes in such things as their time management, their priority activities, and the use of their resources, they are changing and growing. Professor Judy Mansfield at Heritage University has developed several clever and well-accepted metaphors for this. She tells her students they need to "bend their lives." She turns that image away from any negative connotations by using the example of a bow and arrow. The more you bend the bow as you prepare to shoot the arrow, the farther the arrow will fly. In the same way, she challenges students to bend their lives so that they can reach their farthest aspirations, including earning a university diploma. The advantage of this metaphor is that it clearly does not imply that you are supposed to become a different person as you become a successful college student. No, it is still the basic you. She stresses that students have inner strengths and abilities that they have not yet discovered. The only way they will find those is by "bending" to meet the difficult circumstances that arise as part of their new role as university learners. This means recognizing and accepting the assignments that require them to use their inner strengths and resources in new ways. It means accepting challenges and scary tests, even risking failure, so that their own undiscovered talents will come to the fore.

Professor Mansfield points out to students that the pathway they followed through high school was a narrow, defined path of how to do studies that students never deviated from, but that university learning is different. It will require new ways of doing things, new pathways that will unfold as they continue to pursue their degree programs. She tells them that this process will give them a "mental rebirth" based on "using their inner strength in new ways." She keeps reminding them regularly that their dedication to this "bending" will be exciting and enriching, drawing on capacities and abilities they haven't recognized before. Through this kind of input, students are being subtly reprogrammed from a belief that first-gen or low-income students don't do well in college to a new inner belief in themselves and a hopefulness that creates new energy, which leads to accomplishments they previously thought impossible.

A highly respected physician who worked in the Yakima Valley and with the University of Washington before retiring to the East Coast recently wrote to me: "I shall never forget the graduation I attended at Heritage College.[4] I thought those graduating seniors would bring more to the world than those graduating at the same time from Harvard."[5] Dr. Hill recognized that because so few of their family and community members had achieved baccalaureate or higher degrees, every one of them would play a crucial role in the future of their communities. Moreover, since the communities they represent are becoming a larger proportion of our country's citizens, the talent and strengths that he saw these New Majority graduates cultivating will be significant far beyond their own local communities. This is why it is so important that we professors communicate our belief in them and help them become comfortable with their new academic and professional identities.

At the same time, Professor Mansfield's images of "bending" and "following a changing pathway" do not suggest that students should leave behind their families or loved ones. Rather, it communicates that being at the university means they are immersed in a place that expects them to be learning new skills and becoming more competent persons precisely because they are tapping into the inner richness of their own gifts. Growing these talents will allow them to contribute to their own families and communities, a motivation, as I've pointed out previously, that is very strong in working-class students whose families generally steer them toward interdependence and helping others as top priorities.[6] To have the courage to explore and grow unused inner strengths prepares a person to give significant assistance to the needs and dreams of family and society.[7]

Help Students Share Their New Identity

When students become more comfortable thinking of themselves as adopting a new academic identity, they will inevitably think about whether they should share this with their family members. Many are very nervous about having this conversation. They don't want it to be perceived as a way in which the student is implicitly saying, "Look at me. I'm doing all this that you never did. I'm becoming better than you are." Students need help to explore ways they can share their experience of adopting an academic identity in such a way that it is well received and viewed as a positive family accomplishment. This exploration with an individual student, or in class or with small student groups, can include identifying other examples of adopting additional identities to fit into other settings that some family members have already experienced. If any have done military service, this will be a great example. Other involvements in which a family member may have practiced some identity adaptations include participation in various team sports, being a member of a marching band or orchestra, or filling certain roles in a local church. By getting students to talk with each other or with their professor about these parallel examples, before they attempt the conversation at home, students can visualize ways to share with family members that will have positive outcomes.

Emphasize "Academic" Language

One of the places it is most difficult to get New Majority students to adapt to their new academic identity is when writing a paper in which they are encouraged to express their own opinion or when they have to give an oral presentation in public. Problems arise when students use the grammar and vocabulary that reflect the colloquial, geographic, or ethnic language usage perfectly suited to their family or neighborhood settings. If professors respond to these departures from academic writing by telling students "You made a mistake, this is incorrect," the student has to deal with an internal rumination that goes something like this: "But that's the way my parents and all the elders in my family and neighborhood talk. Is the professor saying that they always make mistakes? That they can't talk right? Is he or she putting them down? Will I be implicitly putting them down by changing to the grammar or word that the professor is asking for?"

Using a more effective approach, the professor can bring attention to the same grammar or vocabulary problem in a way that helps support students in adapting to an academic identity in their writing while not making them feel an inner conflict. The professor can say, "What you've used here is informal English. But this is an academic paper, so you have to use academic English."[8] This comment helps the student to see another way in which academic identity should be exercised. It does so while avoiding a distraction for the student, namely, implying that the family language usage—and therefore the family—is inadequate and less than acceptable. When professors adopt this more knowledgeable way of responding to English writing issues, or formal oral presentations, it is one more step in the process of helping first-gen students adopt an academic identity.

Raise Awareness of Other Academic Behaviors

The use of language is one of the most prominent ways in which a person's identity affects behavior in academia. However, it is only one of many subtle behavior traits and implicit rules of interaction that are different for many professors from middle-class backgrounds versus the New Majority students' home cultures. As professors become more sensitive to these differences, they can use informal conversation opportunities—outside class or when meeting students elsewhere on campus—to help them become both adept at and comfortable in their new academic identity. An overt discussion of ways to accomplish contextual shifting could touch on such subtle matters as eye contact in various settings, how to maintain a positive conversational tone while disagreeing with the other speaker, or when and how one can decline a request without being either dishonest or disrespectful. Talking candidly with students about these matters can provide a crucial bridge into the world of academia for first-gen students. Professors John Reveles (California State University, Northridge) and Bryan Brown (Stanford University) have concluded: "Many ethnic and linguistic minority students are not explicitly taught contextual shifting (i.e., changing their ways of speaking, acting, and interacting) . . . [But] as students learn contextual shifting . . . they are better able to appropriate academic identities . . . that will not conflict with their own cultural identities."[9]

SUMMARY

The goal of strategies to help students adopt an academic identity is simply this: increasing the likelihood of students completing their college studies. These strategies also provide many rewarding moments for faculty who take the time and thoughtful planning to incorporate them into their classroom teaching.

As for Martha, after about three years, she finished a two-year certificate program in computer science. During the last term before she finished the certificate, she confided in me that something wonderful had happened which let her know that her father-in-law, who by then was aware of her taking classes but always acted like he didn't know, was actually pleased and proud of Martha's academic accomplishments. It happened at a regional event where Martha's two boys were performing, and her father-in-law was the emcee. At one point he mentioned that he wanted to thank his family for being present, and he said each one's name. When he came to his daughter-in-law Martha, he not only said her name but added, "and we are very proud of her because she has earned a computer science certificate from Heritage University and will be graduating later this spring." Although he never directly made any similar remarks to Martha, this public recognition of her was a clear sign that the whole family rejoiced to witness. And that allowed many of them to attend Martha's graduation the next month. Her commencement was resounding proof that learning to manage both an academic identity and a first-gen, low-income home identity is not only possible but a victory for everyone.

CHAPTER 14

Building Professional Identities to Counter Stereotypes

GABRIELA COULDN'T REMEMBER when she first thought about being an architect, but it must have been when she was still in grade school. It might have been when she was watching the new high school being built in her town with remarkable multi-storied, colored glass walls. Or maybe when her family went back to Mexico to visit her grandparents and they took her to see the modern circular basilica honoring Our Lady of Guadalupe, inspired by the shape of a rose, and holding thousands of pilgrims. "Wouldn't it be great to be able to think up something like that?" she often thought. The majority of her classmates were from Mexican immigrant families like herself, and many of them had also visited family in Mexico City or Morelia or Guadalajara. She loved to see the postcards or photos they brought back that showed the amazing colonial cathedrals or plaza buildings, and these further piqued her interest in being an architect.

Gabriela studied very hard all through her high school junior and senior years, earning almost all A's and taking all the college prep classes, so she would be ready for the university's architecture program. As graduation approached, her friends continued their good-natured teasing because Gaby (their nickname for Gabriela) was very short and looked so young for her age, even though she was eighteen. "Wow! You're really gonna make our school look good! When they see you graduating, they'll say our school's students are so smart that we have fourteen-year-olds who're getting their diplomas!"

No one else in Gaby's family had attended college or earned a degree. Yet her family supported Gaby's aspirations, although it meant she would be moving away from the hometown they all felt comfortable in, so she could enroll in the big university on the other side of the state, the only place she could study architecture. After moving into the dorm, Gaby faced the first day of classes. She found it quite challenging to navigate through several buildings across campus to search out the classroom listed on her schedule for each class. She succeeded in finding the first two morning classes, even getting there early enough to choose a seat and have her textbook out when the professor entered the room. The third class was little more difficult to find, and when she got there the professor was already at the podium, apparently organizing his notes. He looked up at Gaby, who was one of the last students to enter the room, and said, "Come on in! There're still a few seats empty. Welcome to class!" As quickly as she could, she took an empty place, and the professor began his presentation.

After lunch, finding the afternoon class was more challenging. She was looking for the introductory architecture class, listed on her schedule as located in the School of Architecture building on the other side of campus. She finally found the room, saw that the professor was already at the podium, and noticed at least a hundred students already in their seats. Since the door was still open, she stepped inside and tried to eye an empty seat, noticing that the vast majority of students were male, and mostly looked white or Asian American. As she surveyed the rows for a possible seat, she didn't see any Latino/a faces, and as this observation wheedled its way into her consciousness, she tried to quiet her racing brain. She didn't notice the professor glancing up from the lectern, looking over at her.

His voice rose above the quiet murmuring in the room. "Can we help you? Are you lost?"

Gaby was stunned by the question. Why was he asking if she was lost? Why wasn't he welcoming her to the class, the way the professor in the morning had done? She quickly surveyed the students already in their seats, who were all watching her now. All those male students, gazing quizzically at her. And not one person who looked like her. She could feel her face starting to *flush. In a sudden rush of panic it dawned on her what was happening: no one thought she belonged in this room. "But I do belong here," she said to herself. "It's on my schedule." She was starting to feel a little defiant. "Isn't this the Architecture 200 class?" she said aloud. Her voice sounded timid, even to herself.*

The professor appeared surprised, and then caught himself. "Why, yes. It is. Are you registered for this class?"

Gaby immediately started rummaging for her course registration sheet, thinking she would have to prove that she was enrolled. Then she stopped herself, eyeing the professor again, and answered, "Yes, I'm signed up for Architecture 200."

"Well, find yourself a seat," the professor responded and began viewing his notes again. As Gaby walked up the rows of chairs, checking for a place to land, she didn't see anyone who appeared warm or welcoming. Most of them were checking out their new textbook, or talking quietly with their seatmates, or just glancing skeptically at her as she passed by.

Later that day she described the scene to her mother on the phone. "I never felt so unwelcome in my life," she exclaimed. "And it was all because of how I looked to them, 'cuz I hadn't met any of them personally. I wasn't a man, I wasn't white, I wasn't even Asian. And I know I appear really young. They didn't think there was any way I could be an architecture major!"

Many months later, Gaby's mother shared that her daughter frequently mentioned how uncomfortable she felt in that class after her first very difficult day. As Gaby put it, after she had passed that and other courses in the architecture program, "The stereotype they had of who could be an architect was so strong. And I didn't fit that stereotype—no way! During the whole class, I could feel that they kept thinking I wouldn't know how to do the assignments. They were sure I was going to fail. But now that I've passed that class, and I've finished several other architecture pre-reqs with those same students, they're starting to treat me a little better. I'm going to show them that I can be an architect just like them!"

WHAT'S GOING ON HERE?

Now that you have read Gabriela's story, you will be pleased to learn that she is currently in upper-division architecture courses and still doing well. The experience that Gaby had on the first day of her first architecture class might well have discouraged many aspiring students. Fortunately, she was able to overcome that stark experience of stereotype threat.

Two questions emerge as we consider her traumatic experience. First, why was she surprised by the reaction she experienced from both the professor and the students, since she probably knew intellectually that most architects are male and white? Secondly, why was Gaby able to withstand that initially jarring experience, succeed in the class, and continue to pursue her dreams of becoming an architect by remaining in the architecture program? As we know from research about persistence rates, many first-gen students like Gaby would have dropped out.

The surprised and threatened reaction that Gaby felt when the professor asked her if she was lost indicated that she did not expect the reactions of the professor and the students to her appearance at the classroom door. As she approached the classroom, she was focusing on her identity as a freshman university student acting responsibly at the first class of the term by showing up almost on time and with her textbook. In shorthand, she was seeing herself as a university architecture major. The reaction of the professor and the students told her that this was not the identity that they saw at their classroom door. Rather, they seemed to be observing a person who wasn't supposed to be part of the Architecture 200 class. In an instant, Gaby had to adjust her sense of identity so she could respond to what they were seeing. This meant focusing on aspects of her identity that she realized were being interpreted as indications she couldn't be an architecture major: she was a female who looked very young and Hispanic. Seeing this response to her immediately triggered a stereotype threat reaction within her mind. It was evident that she was not expected to be able to succeed in this class, because she wasn't bringing the "right" background to its challenges.

There is an important lesson for us to notice as we analyze her experience. In this incident that lasted less than a minute, from her entrance into the room until she was seated and the professor started the class, Gaby's mind was reprogrammed from a success mindset to a defensive, threatened mindset that would plague her throughout the entire course. In relation to the strategies that will be suggested below, this insight is important because it highlights how significant a stereotype threat situation can be if the person has no expectation that it is likely to happen. It comes as a total shock and surprise. While no professor wants this to happen to a bright, capable student like Gaby, it will undoubtedly happen to some New Majority students both during their university education and again when they enter their first professional experiences. Professors can strategize with students to prepare for such occasions, and thus equip them to deal positively with identity threatening situations.

While Gaby did not have any warning, apparently, that she would be facing this stereotype threat when she showed up at her class, and thus suffered the full initial brunt of that trauma, she was able to move beyond it and succeed in both the class and joining her chosen challenging major. What made her able to do so? Numerous research projects conducted during the past ten years have studied how students can persevere and succeed in spite of experiencing incidents of stereotype and identity threat. Common factors emerging from most of these studies include the importance of having a greater sense of confidence and of belonging at the institution, participating in special programs for first-gen or underrepresented students (such as federally funded Educational Opportunity Programs including TRIO / Student Support Services), and being aware of campus support services.[1] In other words, evidence points to the need for these students to feel direct connections with others in the institution who can provide regular, positive reinforcement for their ability to succeed in college. Much of this happens in the special programs operated beyond professors' classrooms, which are different in each institution. Professors can be instrumental in seeing that their New Majority students participate by staying well informed about these group activities on their campuses and regularly encouraging students to take part in them. This is important in addition to the in-classroom strategies that professors can use to convince students to envision themselves succeeding in their chosen profession and to see their professor as an advocate for this outcome for each of them.[2]

But even with the help provided by these supplemental programs, many New Majority students will still experience communication mismatches with those in the professional settings such as internships or first jobs that students are preparing to enter. They also may have similar mismatches with the professors and/or classmates in the advanced courses in their professional major. The key elements that make these mismatches happen, as a student joins a group in a classroom or in a professional work setting, relate to *expectations* on both sides. On the student's side, he or she is expecting to be included in the new group on the same basis as all the other qualified participants. Students have by this time usually built up confidence and a sense of being competent, to the extent that they are no longer consciously aware of the stereotypes that they will have to deal with. These labels have slipped into a subliminal level, and so students are not prepared to deal with them when they unexpectedly surface. For their part, professors or professional workplace colleagues are immediately and keenly aware of the unique aspects of the new student's identity (gender and/or minority ethnicity and/or working-class status) because persons with this student's identities have rarely been present as competent colleagues or students in the professors' or colleagues' milieu, and so their focus on these identity factors is immediate and unavoidable. And this creates the mismatch. The initial reaction of the professor or of the new professional colleagues comes spontaneously from previous stereotypes or experiences of unqualified persons with those same identities.

In the story about Gaby and her first architecture class, if the student arriving at the last minute to Architecture 200, looking for a seat, had been a white male, it is likely that the professor's spontaneous comment would have been something like "Hurry up and find a seat, I'm about ready to start," or "Who has an empty seat nearby for this last student?" Without thinking about it, the professor's quick comment to Gaby—"Are you lost?"—was based on his automatic subliminal assessment of the stereotypes he had experienced many times in his career as an architect and professor of architecture: young Latina women are not architecture majors.[3] And Gaby's shocked reaction, immediately triggering an unexpected stereotype threat for her, happened because she had been academically successful and had thoroughly proved to herself that she could be a good architecture student, and ultimately an architect, and so she was not consciously aware of her identity aspects—her identity contingencies—that trigger stereotypes.[4]

Earlier in this book we have discussed ways that professors can build student confidence and assist students in dealing with their stereotype threat experiences when these are very much operative in their sense of not belonging. As these students succeed in overcoming those early challenges, they may begin to encounter some additional challenges.

STRATEGIES TO ADDRESS STEREOTYPES IN THE WORKPLACE

The issue of stereotypes and the identity threat that they can produce is important not only for students trying to succeed in college. The challenge will await many New Majority students as they move into professional roles once they have earned their degrees. If their chosen major includes a required internship or practicum, the stereotype concern will likely affect them in these professional settings even before they graduate. Professor Jeff Thompson at Heritage University has devised a very useful multidimensional approach to assist students in facing these challenges, as he teaches psychology majors.

Acknowledge Students as "Future Professionals"

From the first day of class, Professor Thompson refers to his new students as "future professionals." He regularly prefaces information or directives he is sharing with students by starting his comments with, "As future professionals, you need to know / you should be aware that / you will benefit from / I am asking you to . . ." This strategy has a dual purpose. It addresses both the subtle stereotype threat that some students may still be experiencing and the low confidence of many New Majority students. When a student has been in class for several days and has heard himself called a "future professional" five or ten times each day, by the end of the week a subtle positive change in how he envisions himself in relation to his future is likely taking place.[5]

Another aspect of this simple strategy is for the professor to vary which part of the class and which students he looks at as he makes comments, especially those that start with "As future professionals . . ." It is easy to get in the habit of looking only at certain students because they are sitting in front or because of their always-interested facial expressions. Overcoming that tendency and instead deliberately changing the targeted student group each time you look out at the class is a habit that takes some planning and practice. As professors get proficient at including everyone in the class through this nonverbal, eye-contact practice, they will soon begin to see more students either returning their eye contact directly or respectfully looking aside but attentive, depending upon which of these eye-contact behaviors is a communication match with their culture. This inclusive nonverbal contact reinforces that the "future professional" designation is not meant only for a few of the students in the class, but for everyone. Changing this subtle behavior may seem like a minor point, but when we consider how Gaby's stereotype threat was activated for the entire term by only one short statement and glance from the professor, it should be evident why the "future professionals" and concomitant inclusive eye contact are important as ongoing strategies during the whole term. Professors will frequently notice that these subtle additions to their classroom strategies lead to more openness on the part of reserved students. Such students may then initiate or respond positively to friendly short dialogues with the professor as they leave or enter the classroom. This can be a first step to initiating a more substantive conversation with a student to give more concrete positive feedback about a class assignment, special project, or practicum.[6]

Be Candid About Stereotypes

One aspect of stereotypes that makes them especially hard to deal with is that many people feel a strong reticence in talking about them. We generally forget that developing stereotypes about people who are "not us" is a universal human trait and undoubtedly served a good purpose in primitive times when it was very important to recognize immediately "your own kind" so you could avoid those who would likely harm you. In our modern world, that reticence to talk about stereotypes is unfortunate because it adds another layer to the stereotype stigma that students may be experiencing. If there is a stereotype that males are not good at being competent nurses but it is considered impolite to talk about it, the male student entering a nursing science class is faced with a dual dilemma. How does he quiet his own anxiety arising from this stereotype threat, and at the same time not bring it up so he can get support or clarification from the professor or the dominant female fellow students?

Professor Thompson teaches psychology at Heritage University and has developed an effective approach, based on the fact that he is usually looking out at a classroom filled primarily with first-gen, working-class, nonwhite students, where more than half of them are female. He talks directly about stereotypes.[7] He mentions specific settings likely of interest to students majoring in his field in which most of its professionals don't look like the students in his classroom. Students generally are aware of this but often have not thought about what effect that will have on them when they enter those settings for internships or later for their first jobs. After focusing students on the current realities about professionals in their field, he delves more fully into the topic of experiencing stereotypes. He shares in detail one or two experiences he has had in which stereotypes led to reactions from others that made him, or someone with him, or another person they observed experiencing stereotyping, feel very uncomfortable. He then asks if anyone else in the class has experienced anything similar. Several hands immediately go up, and he asks some of them to share their stories. After several stories have been aired, he makes the point that Claude Steele, the eminent social psychologist, puts so well. Some professors may wish to use this quote to convince students of its truth:

> There exists no group on earth that is not negatively stereotyped in some way . . . And when people with these identities . . . are in a situation for which a negative stereotype about their group is relevant, they can feel . . . under pressure not to confirm the stereotype for fear that they will be judged or treated in terms of it. Identity threats like this—contingencies of identity—are part of everyone's life.[8]

This creates an opening for the professor to be candid in helping students identify the aspects of identity that are likely to be what social psychology calls identity contingencies. These are aspects of your identity that are relevant in a given setting; in other settings these aspects may be irrelevant and go unnoticed. For instance, you may have noted in my bio that I belong to an order of Catholic Sisters and have been a nun for more than fifty years. If I were visiting a large convent in Mexico, the "woman" aspect of my identity would be totally irrelevant, since everyone else in the building would also be a woman. However, another aspect of my identity, being Scottish, as visually demonstrated by my freckles and curly hair, would definitely be an identity contingency in the Mexican convent context. It would be noticed, and there would undoubtedly be stereotypes around having that background. Identity contingencies that New Majority students have may lead professionals in the students' chosen fields to presume that they probably aren't really competent, because very few individuals of their ethnicity or gender or working-class background have previously been professionals in that field. Students need to be prepared for those presumptions.

Stress the Power of Professional Writing and Presentation Skills

Professors generally desire to get the writing skills of students up to an acceptable level for the profession they plan to enter. The primary reason for this, as described to me by professors at Heritage University, especially in business and psychology, is that they have consistently seen how professional presentations can rapidly change stereotypes based on how people look. But motivating students to improve writing and presentation skills is often very difficult, especially for those coming from families where writing and professional-level reading are not a part of normal life activities. Professors in various disciplines have often heard, "But this isn't a writing class! Why do I have to rewrite this paper? My paper already answers the question you gave us." So this strategy sparks a level of motivation for students to perfect their academic professional writing skills that is very hard to achieve through simply being a hard grader on assigned papers and presentations.

The strategy is this. Explain to students that in a professional setting colleagues and supervisors tend to judge the level of a person's competence in that profession by how effective their written reports or oral presentations are.[9] This means using professional language and organizing a report's ideas according to standards expected in that professional field. It also means expressing ideas with insight, clarity, and appropriate conciseness. The connection with the discussion of stereotypes becomes clear when Professor Thompson tells students that professionals usually judge how capable a colleague is by the quality of their written and oral reports. Even if your colleagues have a negative stereotype about you as a new professional joining them, because of some aspect of your identity like your age, gender, ethnicity, or working-class background, when they see or hear your very well-done report, they no longer pay attention to the stereotyped facets of your identity. In other words, learn to write and speak in professional ways, and you will overcome any negative stereotypes.[10] When he has finished his initial discussion about perfecting their writing and speaking skills, Professor Thompson adds a statement that is remarkable in the eyes of many of his students: "Each of you will become a competent professional. I want you to be able to compete equally with me and people who look like me." Hearing a middle-aged, middle-class, white male college professor say that to his New Majority students, with great sincerity and an evident commitment to their success, creates an astounding infusion of new energy and motivation in them.[11]

Supply Examples of Role Models with Similar Identities

After a professor has worked with the New Majority students in his class to bring their writing and speaking skills to professional levels, this should be brought to the front of their consciousness anytime they are facing a difficult situation where stereotype contingencies may negatively affect them. For instance, a student going to an internship interview can be reminded that last week she gave a professionally rated report that other professors in the department highly praised. Research has shown that the positive images presented to students don't have to be taken from their own performance. Rather, any mental images that counteract the stereotype will be helpful. An experiment a number of years ago proved that simply reminding women, just before taking a difficult math test, of positive women role models who had done outstanding work in the mathematics field, significantly reduced the effects of stereotype threat that had been evident with them earlier.[12] Professors can collect examples of successful professionals who have similar identity characteristics as their students and who are outstanding in the fields students are preparing to enter. They can find opportunities to mention those individuals and their accomplishments at strategic points in the course where students are feeling overwhelmed or their vulnerability to identity threats is surfacing. An amazing example of how important such a small step can be was reported by Claude Steele when he and colleague Kirsten Stoutemeyer inadvertently learned that simply by reminding women math students that they were Stanford students, their performance dramatically improved.[13]

SUMMARY

All of the above-mentioned strategies, addressing the reality of negative stereotypes that many New Majority students will experience as they move into professional settings, can be combined to enhance substantially the success rates of New Majority students. While this requires some revisions in course delivery, careful planning, and additional research on the part of professors, there is nothing more rewarding than seeing students who appeared to be at risk of not completing the course or internship or degree as they progress from their first hesitant day in class into successful students with well-developed thinking skills, burgeoning professional skills, and the potential of becoming future leaders in the professor's academic field.

■ ■ ■

Through my work in Heritage University's Institute for Student Identity and Success, I have had the privilege of exchanging ideas with a number of professors at Heritage, at Yakima Valley Community College, and at Holy Names University in Oakland, California.[14] They have convinced me that dedicated faculty members, no matter what their academic discipline, are realizing today that New Majority students frequently have greater capacities than we assume. As they recognize this exciting but daunting reality, it motivates professors to keep alert for new insights about ways to respond more fully to the needs of New Majority students. It also sensitizes them to the constant challenge of recognizing communication mismatches that happen inadvertently between themselves and their New Majority students, and between continuing-gen and first-gen students. By parsing these incidents carefully, new possibilities will emerge for increasing the engagement, belongingness, confidence, and visioning of their students. Additional creative and effective strategies that can empower and motivate New Majority students are indeed possible in every class.

This book could easily contain many more chapters. I chose those that are included because they highlight the quintessential elements New Majority students need to achieve their dream of a four-year degree. They need to become *engaged learners*. They must overcome the fear of being out of place with a new sense of *belonging* to their college environment. They have to acquire a realistic sense of how much and what kind of work college courses require while simultaneously gaining *confidence* that with hard work they can meet these requirements. And finally they must develop a *vision* of what a college degree will empower them to do and be.

It is my profound hope that the insights and creative ideas shared in these chapters will inspire professors to go beyond simply trying them. I hope I have encouraged you to create additional approaches especially suited to your students and your subject matter.

Through my collaborations over the past several years with research assistants—all of whom are New Majority students—I have a much deeper belief in the mostly-still-hidden potential of this national resource. I would urge professors to work not only with each other but also with their New Majority students to identify additional challenges and create effective solutions leading to academic success and perseverance. Together you can pinpoint, refine, and adopt workable strategies, share them with fellow professors, and gather data that will clarify which are the most effective practices. By uncovering and publicizing these potential new strategies, we can enable the New Majority leaders of tomorrow to envision and engage in creating a world where all people can confidently belong and work together to prepare a better future for the generations to come.

NOTES

Chapter 1

1. "By 2050 . . . non-Hispanic whites, who made up 67% of the U.S. population in 2005, will make up 47% in 2050. The percentage of Hispanics will rise from 14% of the nation's population in 2005 to 29% in 2050. Blacks were 13% of the population in 2005 and will be roughly the same proportion in 2050. Asians, who were 5% of the population in 2005, will be 9% in 2050"; see Jeffrey S. Passel and D'Vera Cohn, "U.S. Population Projections: 2005–2050," Pew Research Center (February 11, 2008), http://www .pewhispanic.org/2008/02/11/us-population-projections-2005-2050/.

2. Median household income in 2012 for non-Hispanic whites was $68,636, and for non-Hispanic blacks it was $33,321. For Hispanics of any race, median household income was $39,005; see Carmen DeNavas-Walt, Bernadette D. Proctor, and Jessica C. Smith, *Income, Poverty, and Health Insurance Coverage in the United States: 2012* (Washington, DC: US Census Bureau, US Government Printing Office, Current Population Reports, September 2013), 8.

3. College Board, *Trends in Higher Education,* 2013, https://trends.collegeboard .org/student-aid/figures-tables/fed-aid-total-enrollment-and-percentage-receiving-pell-grants-over-time.

4. A new configuration of the Heritage University bridge program in writing, called "Fast Track Writing," was launched during summer 2014. Initially the pass rate was 66%, but as the program was refined, the pass rate in summer 2015 was 95%. A key element in the improved results is requiring the writing of two papers each week during the six-week intensive session, keeping the class size to about ten, as well as strong mentoring by the Writing Center's staff throughout the process. See Paula Collucci and Rachel Flynn, "Peer Tutoring at Heritage University" (Power-Point presentation, Heritage University, May 12, 2015).

5. This approach is problematic, because students are paying for these courses although they do not count toward the total credits required for graduation. In addition, if they are using financial aid such as the Pell Grant, they are burning through one or more of the limited number of terms allowed to receive Pell Grants. This can result in students reaching

their senior year with no eligibility for the very student aid which has sustained them to that point.

6. Nicole M. Stephens, Hazel Rose Markus, Stephanie A. Fryberg, Camille S. Johnson, "Unseen Disadvantage: How American Universities' Focus on Independence Undermines the Academic Performance of First-Generation College Students," *Journal of Personality and Social Psychology* (2012): 1180, doi:10.1037/a0027143.

7. According to a report from the US Department of Education in 2012, for students enrolling in a four-year institution, approximately 73% of white students earned a four-year degree within six years, while only 51% of black students and 51% of Hispanic students completed four-year degrees in the same time period; see Terris Ross et al., *Higher Education: Gaps in Access and Persistence Study*, NCES 2012-046 (Washington, DC: Government Printing Office, US Department of Education, National Center for Education Statistics.)

8. *Pell Institute Fact Sheet: 6-year Degree Attainment Rates for Students Enrolled in Higher Education*, The Pell Institute for the Study of Opportunity in Higher Education website, last modified December 14, 2011, http://www.pellinstitute.org/fact_sheets.shtml.

9. Margaret Cahalan and Laura Perna, *Indicators of Higher Education Equity in the United States* (Washington, DC: The Pell Institute for the Study of Opportunity in Higher Education and the University of Pennsylvania Alliance for Higher Education and Democracy, 2015), 30.

10. Heritage University, *Heritage University: About Heritage / Fast Facts* (2015), http://www.heritage.edu/AboutHeritage/FastFacts.aspx.

11. Anthony P. Carnevale, et al., *Learning While Earning: The New Normal* (Washington, DC: Georgetown University Center on Education and the Workforce, 2015), 1, https://cew.georgetown.edu/wp-content/uploads/Working-Learners-Report.pdf.

12. John Bassett, PhD, started his career in higher education as a faculty member at Wayne State University in Detroit, Michigan, then became chair of the English Department at North Carolina State University in Raleigh, and later the dean of arts and sciences at Case Western Reserve University in Cleveland, Ohio. He served for ten years as president of Clark University in Worcester, Massachusetts, before becoming Heritage University's second president in 2010.

13. Institute for Higher Education Policy, *Supporting First-Generation College Students Through Classroom-Based Practices* (Washington, DC: IHEP Issue Brief, 2012).

14. The *Breakthrough Strategies Videos* were professionally produced for us from scripts we developed with Marie Strohm, President of Hummingbird

Productions. They are available for free viewing through the link at www .heritage.edu/institute or directly at https://www.youtube.com/user/ HeritageISIS/videos?view=0&sort=dd&shelf_id=0.

15. "The probability (p value) that the distributions we are seeing would be a chance occurrence is only .017 (less than .05)." E-mail with subject "Interpretation of chi-square results" from Nina Oman, Heritage University Director of Institutional Effectiveness, to Kathleen Ross on January 28, 2015.

16. The website for the Heritage University Center for Intercultural Learning and Teaching may be viewed at http://www.heritage.edu/FacultyStaff/ CILTResourcesforFaculty.aspx. Anyone may access it and utilize the many useful materials available.

Chapter 2

1. For a wealth of information on colleges that have closed, see the very robust website College History Garden at http://collegehistorygarden.blog spot.com/2014/11/index-of-colleges-and-universities-that.html.

2. A full history of Fort Wright College of the Holy Names is recorded in the out-of-print publication by Letitia Mary Lyons SNJM, *A Chronicle of Holy Names Normal, Holy Names College and Fort Wright College of the Holy Names, 1907-1982* (Spokane, WA: University Press, 1984).

3. Yakima County's Hispanics formed just 14.8% of the population in 1980 but had expanded to a whopping 47.7% of the county's population by 2014; see Carmen DeNavas-Walt, Bernadette D. Proctor, and Jessica C. Smith, *Income, Poverty, and Health Insurance Coverage in the United States: 2012* (Washington, DC: US Census Bureau, US Government Printing Office, Current Population Reports, September 2013 P60–245).

4. In 2012, approximately 35% of students enrolled in four-year public or nonprofit colleges nationally received federal Pell Grants; see *Digest of Education Statistics* (Washington, DC: Institute of Education Sciences, National Center for Education Statistics, 2014), https://nces.ed.gov/pro grams/digest/d14/tables/dt14_331.20.asp.

Chapter 3

1. John Regan, "Mis-Match in Communications" (unpublished manuscript, Claremont, CA: Claremont Graduate University, 1978).

2. Kathleen Anne Ross (doctoral dissertation, Claremont, CA: Claremont Graduate University / University Microfilms International, 1979; UMI #7911543); dissertation received the Peter Lincoln Spencer Award for Outstanding Doctoral Dissertation in Education from Phi Delta Kappa, Claremont, California.

3. Richard W. Brislin, et al., *Intercultural Interactions: A Practical Guide* (Newbury Park, CA: Sage Publications, 1986), 13.
4. Clotaire Rapaille, *The Culture Code* (New York: Broadway Books, 2006), 5–6.
5. Professor Regan developed a complete categorization system for all types of communication interactions between individuals. The only published place that I am aware of where this system is available in print is in my dissertation; see Ross (1979), 40–50.
6. Candia Elliot, R. Jerry Adams, and Suganya Sockalingam, "Communication Patterns and Assumptions of Differing Cultural Groups in the United States," *Multicultural Toolkit Summary,* January 1, 2016, http://www.awesome library.org/multiculturaltoolkit-patterns.html.
7. Harold V. B. Gilliam and Sjef Van Den Berg, "Communication Research Program: University of Connecticut," *Urban Education* 15 (April 1980): 84.
8. Carol Barnhardt uncovered this problem in her early research in a Native Alaskan village; see Carol Barnhardt, "Tuning In: Athabaskan Teachers and Athabaskan Students," *Cross-Cultural Issues in Alaskan Education* (Fairbanks, AK: University of Alaska Fairbanks, Center for Cross-Cultural Studies, 1982). See also her article "Life on the Other Side: Native Student Survival in a University World," *Peabody Journal of Education* 69, no. 2 (Winter 1994).
9. Eric Law, author of several books on effective communication in multicultural groups, invented a method for group discussion which solves this issue. He calls it "Mutual Invitation," in which the group leader calls on someone to speak, who then calls on the next speaker when he has finished speaking or says "pass." This process continues until every person has both been called on and has called on another. More detail is available in Eric Law, *The Wolf Shall Dwell with the Lamb* (Danvers, MA: Chalice Press, 1993).

Chapter 4

1. Claude M. Steele, *Whistling Vivaldi: How Stereotype Threats Affect Us and What We Can Do* (New York: W. W. Norton, 2010), 5.
2. Anne Krendl, et al., "The Negative Effects of Threat: A Functional Magnetic Resonance Imaging Investigation of the Neural Mechanisms Underlying Women's Underperformance in Math," *Psychological Science* 19, no. 2 (2008): 168.
3. T. Schmader and M. Johns, "Convergent Evidence That Stereotype Threat Reduces Working Memory Capacity," *Journal of Personality and Social Psychology* 85 (2003): 440–452.
4. Fergus I. M. Craik, "Effects of Distraction on Memory and Cognition:

A Commentary," *Frontiers in Psychology* 5 (2014): 841, doi:10.3389/fpsyg .2014.00841.

5. Geoff L. Cohen, Claude M. Steele, and Lee D. Ross, "The Mentor's Dilemma: Providing Critical Feedback Across the Racial Divide," *Personality and Social Psychology Bulletin* 25 (1999): 1302–18. Also Geoff L. Cohen, et al., "Reducing the Racial Achievement Gap: A Social-Psychological Intervention," *Science* 313 (September 2006): 1307–10.

6. Steele, *Whistling*, 163.

7. Unfortunately, only 26% of the college and university presidents are women as of 2014. Lucie Lapovsky, "Why So Few Women College Presidents?," *Forbes* (April 13, 2014), http://www.forbes.com/sites/lucielapovsky/2014/ 04/13/why-so-few-women-college-presidents/#5b1ebdd9634c.

8. You can hear Professor James talk about how she uses her feedback process with students in a 3-minute video available at https://www.youtube .com/watch?v=angMump9ymA.

9. Philip Uri Treisman, "Studying Students Studying Calculus: A Look at the Lives of Minority Mathematics Students in College," *College Mathematics Journal* 23 (1992): 362–72.

10. See discussion in chapter 9 about interdependence versus independence in collegiate settings.

Chapter 5

1. Professor Maria Cuevas's 4-minute video describing her strategy which she calls "Power Reading" may be viewed at https://www.youtube.com/ watch?v=XxKStM6xFAw.

2. "There is a clear relationship between stress and cognitive functioning as assessed by laboratory-based measures of cognition," from Adriel Boals and Jonathan B. Banks, "Effects of Traumatic Stress and Perceived Stress on Everyday Cognitive Functioning," *Cognition and Emotion* 26, no. 7 (2012): 1336.

3. "The use of appropriate content-related humor can initiate and liberate thinking, reduce academic anxiety, promote the retention of academic material, and increase student satisfaction," from Patti Garrett and Rick Shade, "The Laughter-Learning Link," *Science Scope* 27, no. 8 (May 2004): 27.

4. "Think Pair Share," Carlton College: Science Education Resource Center, n.d., http://serc.carleton.edu/introgeo/interactive/tpshare.html.

5. Chapter 10 discusses some ways for professors to make themselves more approachable outside of class time.

6. Rebecca D. Cox, *The College Fear Factor: How Students and Professors Misunderstand One Another* (Cambridge, MA: Harvard University Press, 2009).

7. Rebecca Cox reports hearing exactly this criticism of one of the professors

she observed in the classroom and whom she considered to be an excellent instructor. When students were put into small groups with very thought-provoking questions, the students told Cox later that the professor "isn't doing her job"; see Cox, *College Fear Factor*, chapter 5.

8. I particularly recommend a short piece that describes very cogently the resistance students from immigrant populations may be feeling to asking questions. It is written by Laura Gutierrez Spencer at New Mexico State University: Laura G. Spencer, "Classroom Tips for Faculty Working with First Generation and Minority Students," Faculty Development Handouts (Las Cruces, NM: New Mexico State University, 2012), 4, http://nmsua .edu/files/uploads/sites/2/2014/08/classroom-tips-titlev.pdf.

Chapter 6

1. Patricia Ann deWinstanley and Robert A. Bjork, "Successful Lecturing: Presenting Information in Ways that Engage Effective Processing," in *New Directions for Teaching and Learning* (Wiley Periodicals 89, 2002).
2. Several studies shed light on how being focused in learning situations—which happens with a vivid story or mental picture such as George created about the marathon—reduces stress. See, for example, Aslak Hjeltnes, et al., "Facing the Fear of Failure: An Explorative Qualitative Study of Client Experiences in a Mindfulness-based Stress Reduction Program for University Students with Academic Evaluation Anxiety," *U.S. National Library of Medicine* (August 20, 2015), http://www.ncbi.nlm.nih.gov/pmc/ articles/PMC4545197/.
3. Lori Arviso Alvord and Elizabeth Cohen Van Pelt, *The Scalpel and the Silver Bear* (New York: Bantam Books, 1999), 27.
4. deWinstanley and Bjork, "Successful Lecturing," 20.
5. Ibid. Also see Dr. Barcena's marathon analogy at www.heritage.edu/ institute.
6. Martin Luther King Jr. (1957), http://www.mlkonline.net/enemies.html.
7. Martin Luther King Jr., *Noble Prize Acceptance Speech* (1964), http://www .nobelprize.org/nobel_prizes/peace/laureates/1964/king-acceptance.html.
8. Ibid.
9. My matrix description is based on a process for developing analogies described in Janis A. Bulgren, et al., "The Use and Effectiveness of Analogical Instruction in Diverse Secondary Content Classrooms," *Journal of Educational Psychology* 92 (2000): 426–41.
10. Carol M. Donnelly and Mark A. McDaniel, "Analogy with Knowledgeable Learners: When Analogy Confers Benefits and Exacts Costs," *Psychonomic Bulletin and Review*, 7 (2000): 537–43.
11. Greta G. Freeman and Pamela D. Wash, "You Can Lead Students to the

Classroom, and You Can Make Them Think: Ten Brain-based Strategies for College Teaching and Learning Success," *Journal on Excellence in College Teaching* 24, no. 3 (2013): 100.

12. Ken Bain, *What the Best College Teachers Do* (Cambridge, MA: Harvard University Press, 2004), 39–40.

Chapter 7

1. See Claude M. Steele, *Whistling Vivaldi: How Stereotypes Affect Us and What We Can Do* (New York: W. W. Norton, 2010), 89–98.

2. Laura G. Spencer, "Classroom Tips for Faculty Working with First Generation and Minority Students," Faculty Development Handouts (Las Cruces, NM: New Mexico State University, 2012), 1.

3. Ibid.

4. Professor Rousculp and several Heritage University colleagues and students were chosen by the Association of American Colleges and Universities to participate in a 2012 workshop on "High Impact Practices," and the Text Hunt exercise reflects the ideas explored in this institute.

5. You can view Professor Rousculp's description of how he uses the Text Hunt in a 3-minute video available at https://www.youtube.com/watch?v=OHVQsXBb8U4.

6. Paul Lingenfelter, president of the State Higher Education Executive Officers Association, noted the importance of "employing 'high-impact' instructional practices, with or without technology, that more deeply engage students in creative work to develop the skills they will need as professionals and citizens"; see "American Education Second to None? How We Must Change to Meet Twenty-First-Century Imperatives," *Liberal Education* 99 (Spring 2013), http://www.aacu.org/publications-research/periodicals/american-education-second-none-how-we-must-change-meet-twenty.

7. Mark Canada, "The Syllabus: A Place to Engage Students' Egos," *New Directions for Teaching and Learning* (Wiley On-Line Library, 2013), 40, www.wileyonlinelibrary.com. Professor Canada has a number of useful and practical suggestions in this article about writing a syllabus that students will relate to and use.

8. "Some students enter higher education with an unrealistic expectation that they will be provided with all the information they are required to learn, and do not expect to have to engage in independent study . . . [These] factors predict student withdrawal." Laura Nicholson, et al., "The Key to Successful Achievement as an Undergraduate Student: Confidence and Realistic Expectations?" *Studies in Higher Education* 38, no. 2 (March 2013): 285.

Chapter 8

1. Lee Ward, Michael J. Siegel, and Zebulun Davenport, *First Generation College Students* (San Francisco: Jossey-Bass, 2012), 7.
2. Collier and Morgan detail additional examples of different expectations regarding college in Peter J. Collier and David L. Morgan, "'Is That Paper Really Due Today?' Differences in First-generation and Traditional College Students' Understandings of Faculty Perspectives," *Higher Education* 55 (2000): 425–26.
3. A good reference for describing various communication theories, especially as they relate to cross-cultural situations, is this classic work, in its second edition: William B. Gudykunst and Bella Mody, *Handbook of International and Intercultural Communication* (Thousand Oaks, CA: Sage Publications, 2001).
4. The Institute for Student Identity and Success at Heritage University conducted almost 100 informal student-to-student interviews during 2012–2014 to surface barriers for first-generation students and to identify professors who employed helpful strategies to address these barriers. These comments are among those collected during the interviews.
5. Lynn Jacobs and Jeremy Hyman, *The Secrets of College Success*, 2nd ed. (San Francisco: Wiley Press, 2013), chapter 3. For some additional specific approaches, see Amy G. Lahmers and Chen R. Zulauf, "Factors Associated with Academic Time Use and Academic Performance of College Students: a Recursive Approach," in *Journal of College Student Development* 41, no. 5 (2000): 544.
6. Rebecca Cox's interviews with community college students, most of whom were first-gen, revealed that "students [had] narrowly defined conceptions of 'college' instruction . . . Many students, for instance, defined instruction that was not delivered in the form of a lecture as no instruction whatsoever. Students appreciated the professors' expert knowledge and thought of the instructors' primary task as one of explaining the information clearly." This meant that time given in class to discussion groups was viewed by these students as the professor being lazy and not fulfilling his or her job; see Rebecca D. Cox, *The College Fear Factor: How Students and Professors Misunderstand One Another* (Cambridge, MA: Harvard University Press, 2009), 160.
7. Cathy Engstrom and Vincent Tinto, "Access Without Support Is Not Opportunity," *Change* (January–February, 2008): 46–50.
8. Marcia Roe-Clark, "Succeeding in the City: Challenges and Best Practices on Urban Commuter Campuses," *About Campus* (2006): 7.
9. Paula S. Wise, "Book Review: Brophy, Jere (2004) Motivating Students to Learn," *School Psychologist* (2005): 35. The book reviewed is Jere Brophy,

Motivating Students to Learn (Mahwah, NJ: Lawrence Erlbaum Associates, 2004).

10. Roe-Clark, "Succeeding," 4.
11. Marcia Roe-Clark, "Negotiating the Freshman Year: Challenges and Strategies Among First-Year College Students," *Journal of College Student Development* 46 (2005): 296–316.

Chapter 9

1. Nicole M. Stephens, Hazel Rose Markus, Stephanie A. Fryberg, Camille S. Johnson, "Unseen Disadvantage: How American Universities' Focus on Independence Undermines the Academic Performance of First-Generation College Students," *Journal of Personality and Social Psychology* (2012): 1178–1179, doi:10.1037/a0027143.
2. Ibid., 1178.
3. Ibid., 1179.
4. Ibid., 1181.
5. Ibid.
6. Patrick T. Terenzini, et al., "The Transition to College: Diverse Students, Diverse Stories," *Research in Higher Education,* no. 35 (1994): 57–73, doi:10.1007/BF02496662.
7. You can hear Professor Elese Washines talk about this strategy in a 3-minute video available at https://www.youtube.com/watch?v=t4ad36ppR-0.
8. Rebecca D. Cox, *The College Fear Factor: How Students and Professors Misunderstand One Another* (Cambridge, MA: Harvard University Press, 2009), chapter 8.
9. T. Baker and J. Clark, "Cooperative Learning—a Double-edged Sword: A Cooperative Learning Model for Use with Diverse Student Groups," *Intercultural Education* 21, no. 3 (2010): 257–68.

Chapter 10

1. Sujata Gupta, "QnAs with Carol Dweck," *Proceedings of the National Academy of Sciences of the United States of America* 110, no. 37 (2013): 14818.
2. Carol Dweck, *Mindset: The New Psychology of Success* (New York: Ballantine Books, 2008).
3. Another very engaging and informative article on the mindset issue may be found in Marina Krakovsky, "The Effort Effect," *Stanford Magazine* (Stanford University Alumni, Palo Alto, CA, 2007), March/April.
4. The sports example should be carefully chosen; it needs to be one in which the professor was ultimately able to perform at least at a minimally acceptable level, and not one in which s/he remained inept. Otherwise an inadvertent message to students with little academic self-confidence might

be that their lack of self-assurance forebodes an inability to be successful.

5. You can hear Professor Cruz describe his strategies to build student confidence in a 4-minute video available at https://www.youtube.com/watch?v=56VVqEpWe9o.

6. A good description of approaches to self-efficacy and self-confidence strategies is found in Heidi Fencl and Karen Scheel, "Engaging Students," *Journal of College Science Teaching* 35, no. 1 (September 2005): 20–24.

7. American Psychological Association, "Teaching Tip Sheet: Self-Efficacy," February 2016, http://www.apa.org/pi/aids/resources/education/self-efficacy.aspx.

Chapter 11

1. J. P. Charlton, C. Barrow, and A. Hornsby-Atkinson, "Attempting to Predict Withdrawal from Higher Education Using Demographic, Psychological, and Education Measures," *Research in Post-Compulsory Education* 11, no. 1 (2006): 31–47.

2. Laura Nicholson, et al., "The Key to Successful Achievement as an Undergraduate Student: Confidence and Realistic Expectations?" *Studies in Higher Education* 38, no. 2 (March 2013): 286.

3. See chapter 5 in Rebecca D. Cox, *The College Fear Factor: How Students and Professors Misunderstand One Another* (Cambridge, MA: Harvard University Press, 2009), for a detailed description of this dramatic communication mismatch between a composition professor and her students.

4. Cox, *Fear Factor*, 160.

5. Sara Cartmel describes her approach in a 4-minute video available at www.youtube.com/watch?v=MkQmdS95KYg.

6. Rebecca Cox reports on several conversations with students in the courses she was observing in which these simple phrases or comments on a student's paper were reported later to be significant in giving the student the confidence to persevere. See chapter 5 in Cox, *Fear Factor*.

7. Ricardo Valdez, "Relationships Between First Generation College Students and Faculty: A Case Study of a Small Rural Private University" (EdD dissertation, University of Washington, 2016).

8. Ibid., 96.

9. Ibid., 99.

Chapter 12

1. See Krista M. Soria and Michael J. Stebleton, "First-generation Students' Engagement and Retention," *Teaching in Higher Education* 17, no. 6 (2015): 32–41, http://dx.doi.org/10.1080/13562517.2012.666735.

2. "The cultural capital possessed by the middle and upper classes constitutes the invisible curriculum in higher education," Soria and Stebleton,

"First-generation Students," 32. The "invisible curriculum" refers to information and skills that are useful for college success but are usually presumed without being explicitly taught.

3. "Something like this happened . . . to all of the participants under stereotype threat . . . [t]heir minds race, their blood pressure rises, they begin to sweat, they redouble their efforts, they try to refute the stereotype in their own minds and what they can't refute they try to suppress, the brain activity that underlies vigilance to threat increases, and this further suppresses the brain activity critical to performance and functioning." Claude M. Steele, *Whistling Vivaldi: How Stereotypes Affect Us and What We Can Do* (New York: W. W. Norton, 2010), 126.

4. Laura I. Rendón, Romero E. Jalomo, and Amoury Nora, "Theoretical Considerations in the Study of Minority Student Retention in Higher Education," in *Reworking the Student Departure Puzzle*, ed. John M. Braxton (Nashville, TN: Vanderbilt University, 2002), as quoted in Rebecca D. Cox, *The College Fear Factor: How Students and Professors Misunderstand One Another* (Cambridge, MA: Harvard University Press, 2009), 127.

5. Patrick T. Terenzini, et al., "The Transition to College: Diverse Students, Diverse Stories," *Research in Higher Education* 35 (1994): 57–73.

6. A 4-minute video in which Professor Tom Mount describes his seminar strategy is available at https://www.youtube.com/watch?v=nJc6IBWHztI.

7. A 4-minute video featuring Professor Paula Collucci explaining her recording strategy is available at https://www.youtube.com/watch?v=i454Nc3VaQ4.

Part Four

1. George D. Kuh, *High-Impact Educational Practices: What They Are, Who Has Access to Them, and Why They Matter* (Washington, DC: American Association of Colleges and Universities – National Initiative Report 2008).

2. Kuh, *High-Impact*, 10–11.

Chapter 13

1. Those readers who are familiar with the literature related to *identity* will note that I am not discussing here the more detailed aspects of the psychological or linguistic or cultural exploration of identity. If you are interested, see for example Jaan Valsiner, *An Invitation to Cultural Psychology* (London: Sage, 2013). For an exhaustive review of identity in relation to language usage, see Maurizio Gotti, *Linguistic Insights*, vol. 150, *Academic Identity Traits: A Corpus-Based Investigation* (Bern: Peter Lang AG, 2012).

2. Jane Tapp, "'I actually listened, I'm proud of myself.' The Effects of a Participatory Pedagogy on Students' Constructions of Academic Identities," *Teaching in Higher Education* 19, no. 4 (2014): 325.

3. See John M. Reveles and Bryan A. Brown, "Contextual Shifting: Teachers Emphasizing Students' Academic Identity to Promote Scientific Literacy," *Science Education* 92, no. 6 (November 2008): 1015–41. These authors share a useful application of this idea to science classrooms.

4. Heritage College became Heritage University in 2004.

5. Dr. Sherman Hill, MD, Concord, MA, in a private communication, December 2013.

6. See chapter 9 for a further discussion of this value system that is especially important to working-class students.

7. To hear Professor Mansfield describe how she encourages an "academic identity" you can view a 4-minute video at https://www.youtube.com/watch?v=3EIkMTKCs6c.

8. If the student is from an ethnicity or nationality that accounts for the nonacademic English words or grammar in question, the professor might want to acknowledge that by using another term besides "informal English," such as "Spanglish" or "Black English." I would also immediately add a positive comment about the linguistic practice in its natural setting, such as, "That's Spanglish, not academic English. Spanglish helps a lot when you're speaking with people whose first language is Spanish! But you are writing a paper that requires academic English, so please change this."

9. Reveles and Brown, "Contextual Shifting," 1016.

Chapter 14

1. The following studies are indicative of the many resources that address the issues of belonging, confidence, and support services: Greta Winograd and Jonathan P. Rust, "Stigma, Awareness of Support Services, and Academic Help-Seeking Among Historically Underrepresented First-Year College Students," *Learning Assistance Review* 19, no. 2 (2014): 17–41; Gregory M. Walton and Geoffrey L. Cohen, "A Brief Social-belonging Intervention Improves Academic and Health Outcomes of Minority Students," *Science* 331 (2011): 1447–51; Michael J. Stebleton and Krista M. Soria, "Breaking Down Barriers: Academic Obstacles of First Generation Students at Research Universities," *Learning Assistance Review* 17 (2012): 7–20; Michael L. Laskey and Carole J. Hetzel, "Investigating Factors Related to Retention of At-Risk College Students," *Learning Assistance Review* 16 (2011): 31–43; Alberta M. Gloria, et al., "African American Students' Persistence at a Predominantly White University: Influence of Social Support, University Comfort, and Self-Beliefs," *Journal of College Student Development* 40 (1999): 257–268.

2. In the language of the social psychologist, Claude Steele, "If you want to change the behaviors and outcomes associated with social identity—say,

too few women in computer science—don't focus on changing the internal manifestations of the identity, such as values, and attitudes. Focus instead on changing the contingencies [i.e., cues in an environment that indicate particular stereotypes are operative] to which all of that internal stuff is an adaptation"; see *Whistling Vivaldi: How Stereotype Threats Affect Us and What We Can Do* (New York: W. W. Norton, 2010), 81.

3. "The reality of stereotype threat [makes] the point that places like classrooms, university campuses, standardized-testing rooms, or competitive-running tracks, though seemingly the same for everybody, are, in fact, different places for different people," Steele, *Whistling*, 60.

4. "What raises a characteristic we have to a social identity we have are the contingencies that go with the characteristic, most often threatening contingencies," Steele, *Whistling*, 74.

5. Laura Nicholson, et al., "The Key to Successful Achievement as an Undergraduate Student: Confidence and Realistic Expectations?" *Studies in Higher Education* 38, no. 2 (March 2013): 285–98.

6. See chapter 4 for additional strategies regarding effective feedback for students with low confidence or stereotype threat challenges.

7. Nilanjana Dasgupta, "Ingroup Experts and Peers as Social Vaccines Who Inoculate the Self-Concept: The Stereotype Inoculation Model," *Psychological Inquiry* 22 (2011): 231–46.

8. Steele, *Whistling*, 88–89.

9. James P. Coyle, "Teaching Writing Skills That Enhance Student Success in Future Employment," *Collected Essays on Learning and Teaching* 3 (2010): 195–200.

10. Sarah M. Ovink, "More Than 'Getting Us Through': A Case Study in Cultural Capital Enrichment of Underrepresented Minority Undergraduates," *Research in Higher Education* 52 (2011): 370–94.

11. You can hear Professor Thompson describing his approach in a 4-minute video at https://www.youtube.com/watch?v=5nwSDerIC-o&list=UU9k HMl1fr8uGxezYyF3eqjQ.

12. Rusty B. McIntyre, et al., "Alleviating Women's Mathematics Stereotype through Salience of Group Achievement," *Journal of Experimental Social Psychology* 39 (2002): 83–90.

13. Steele, *Whistling*, 94.

14. The Institute for Student Identity and Success professionally produced fourteen 3–4 minute videos, each describing a Breakthrough Strategy. Some have been referenced in earlier chapters. To see links to each of the videos, go to www.heritage.edu/institute. Or go directly to the YouTube site where all 14 are posted together: https://www.youtube.com/user/HeritageISIS/videos?view=0&sort=dd&shelf_id=0.

ACKNOWLEDGMENTS

Turning a single-campus research project into a book intended for professors at campuses across the country was not something I initially imagined I could do. It happened because of the insights and persuasive powers of Caroline Chauncey, assistant director of the Harvard Education Press, and her colleague Nancy Walser. Transforming the content of the short "Breakthrough Strategies" videos that I had produced, based on students' peer interviews, into a full volume still seemed overwhelming until I felt the enthusiastic support of Heritage University's president John Bassett and my faculty colleagues energizing and motivating me. A number of faculty from Heritage University (Nina Barcenas, Sara Cartmel, Paula Collucci, Ernesto "Charro" Cruz, Olivia Gutierrez, Mary James, Judy Mansfield, Michael Parra, Edwin Rousculp, Jeffrey Thompson, Elese Washines) and from Yakima Valley Community College (Maria Cuevas, Tom Mount, Dan Peters) shared creative teaching approaches and provided the springboard for extended research and additional innovative ideas. I am especially indebted to my part-time but always available assistant director for the Institute for Student Identity and Success, Deb Wingood, for her invaluable editing skills and thoughtful questions.

The seeds for this project first sprouted when I was a visiting research professor at Claremont Graduate University in 2011 with the thoughtful insights and encouragement of my colleagues, especially Daryl Smith, Jack Schuster, Scott Thomas, John Regan, and Mary Poplin. They, along with Michelle Asha Cooper, president of the Institute for Higher Education Policy, asked the right questions and kept me on a focused path. My research assistants, funded by the College Spark Washington Foundation and the Sisters of the Holy Names of Jesus and Mary, provided the raw material for many of the strategies described in this book. Thank you to Laura Aguiar, Kristine Cody, Alejandra Cruz,

Vicky Gonzalez, Brandy Jones, Carmen Perez, Lisa Golding, Olivia Marquez, Laurie Robledo, Sam Small, and Mattie Tomeo-Palmanteer for their openness to being challenged and for growing into competent, ingenious researchers.

I was fortunate to reconnect with an outstanding media producer, Marie Strohm, and her company, Hummingbird Productions. Their top-notch professional skills, real passion for New Majority students, and inventiveness in filming, editing, and coining the phrase "Breakthrough Strategies," epitomize the goals of this book. None of this would have been possible without my two cofounders of Heritage University—Violet Lumley Rau (deceased 1994), and Martha Yallup, who continues to motivate and inspire me.

Personal family and friends have been a tremendous support, especially when writing and research have kept me from being present as often as I would like. As a member of the Sisters of the Holy Names of Jesus and Mary (SNJM), I'm especially grateful for our mission of education for the full development of the human person, an inspiration underlying the Breakthrough Strategies work. Special thanks to my housemates, Marina Rose Parisi, SNJM, and Charlyne Brown, SNJM; long-time friend Margaret Kennedy, SNJM; my teammates on the Congregational Leadership Team based in Longueuil, Quebec; and the Sisters and Associates of the SNJM Yakima Mission Centre. I have long cherished the warm friendship and example of dedication to writing regardless of age from my senior friend in Scranton, Pennsylvania, Sister Michel Keenan, IHM. To my dear sister Rosemary Ross, and to Paula Christy, Virginia Hislop, the Garvin family, and the Cockrill family: thank you for being a support system which I will always treasure. To all those other friends and colleagues who have encouraged and supported this project, too numerous to mention, you know who you are. Thank you once again for your friendship, insights, and faithful support.

ABOUT THE AUTHOR

Kathleen A. Ross is President Emerita and Professor of Cross-Cultural Communication at Heritage University, a four-year institution that she founded with two Yakama Indian women in 1982 and led for twenty-eight years. Located in Toppenish on the Yakama Nation Reservation in central Washington State, Heritage University started with 75 students and has grown into a fully accredited, independent university with 1,200 students and more than 8,000 four-year and master degree graduates. Today its undergraduates are approximately 10 percent Native American, 55–60 percent Latino/a, 85 percent first-generation, and more than 80 percent low-income. Dr. Ross has served on many boards including the Congressional Advisory Committee on Student Financial Aid, the National Association of Independent Colleges and Universities (NAICU), and the Northwest Commission on Colleges and Universities (the regional accreditation body). Currently she serves as director of Heritage University's Institute for Student Identity and Success, focused on increasing retention and graduation for first-generation students. She holds a masters degree from Georgetown University (history), and a doctorate from Claremont Graduate University (higher education and cross-cultural communication). Her work has received recognition in the form of numerous awards, including the Harold W. McGraw Education Prize (1989), a MacArthur Fellowship (1997), and fourteen honorary doctorates. In 2012 she celebrated her Golden Jubilee (fifty years) as a Sister of the Holy Names of Jesus and Mary (SNJM). She currently lives in Toppenish, Washington, with two other Holy Names Sisters.

INDEX